Science Panorama 6

Chemistry

Series Editor

Lipika Dutta

Collins

Science Panorama 6

Chemistry

Series Editor
Lipika Dutta

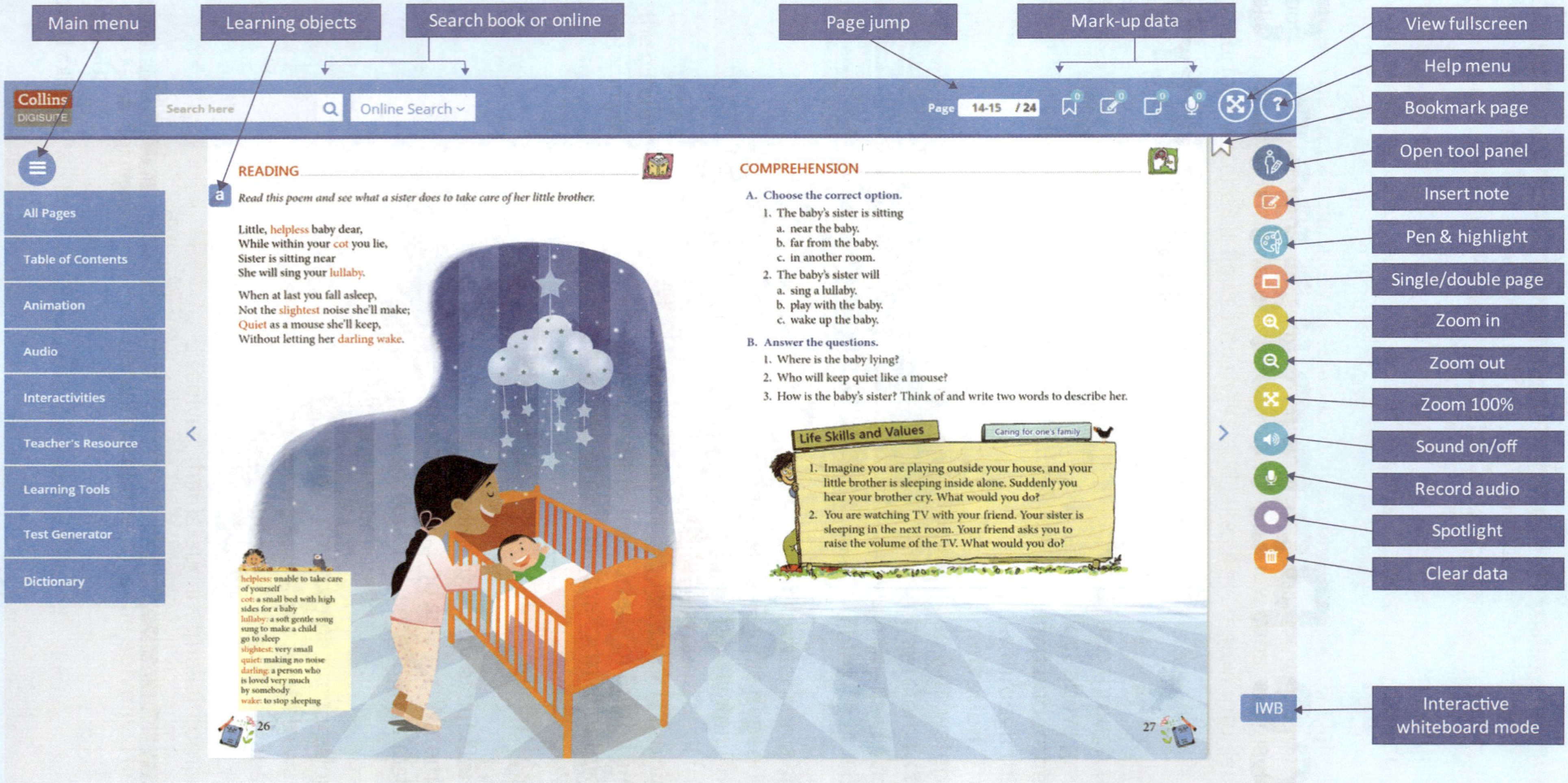

Student + Teacher

- **a** animations
- **ilt** instructor-led tutorials
- **ia** activities
- **w** worksheets
- audio
- **g** games
- **v** videos

Teacher-only

- **lp** lesson plans
- **w** worksheets
- **tn** teacher's notes
- **ak** answer keys

Preface

Science Panorama is a series of books for Classes 1 to 8, which includes 3 books each for Physics, Chemistry and Biology for middle school. The middle school series has been updated based on the **new syllabus** prescribed by the **Council for the Indian School Certificate Examinations**. In line with the new syllabus, a thematic, coherent and structured approach has been followed and all the new topics suggested in the syllabus have been included. Chapter-wise worksheets have also been provided to effectively integrate subject knowledge and life skills for overall development.

This updated edition also emphasizes on developing scientific skills such as observation, investigation, analysis, research and other inferential skills. It focuses on development of concepts as well as their application in real life. Sufficient examples from everyday life have been provided to help learners understand the concepts using age-appropriate language. Colourful illustrations and well-labelled diagrams have been included to engage learners and aid their understanding.

Some Key Features

Science in Context: Additional information on the topic being taught

Do You Know? Interesting facts related to the given topic

Challenge Yourself: Questions testing students' ability to reason and extrapolate

Activities: Individual/collaborative activities to hone experimental and deduction skills

Know the Scientist: Famous scientists and their contribution to the topic at hand

Greenathon: Some tips to keep the environment clean and green

Revision Zone: In-text questions for assessing progress in the course of learning

Keywords: Important terms from the chapter along with their definitions

In a Nutshell: Summary of the chapter content

Exercise: Variety of questions given at the end of each chapter

Subject Integration Worksheets: To effectively integrate knowledge across subjects

Life Skills Worksheets: To create awareness, empathy and a positive attitude towards self and others

Assessment papers: Two assessment papers at the end of the book for effective evaluation

We would like to take this opportunity to thank all the teachers who reviewed the books and provided their valuable feedback, which helped in improving the quality of the content.

Any suggestions or constructive criticism from the users are welcome. We shall try to incorporate those in the future editions.

Authors

Key Features

Do You know?

Interesting facts related to the given topic

Do You Know?

Pieces of pumice rocks can float on water. This is because the air pores in them make the stone less dense than water. This helps e stone to float for a ...as after a wh...

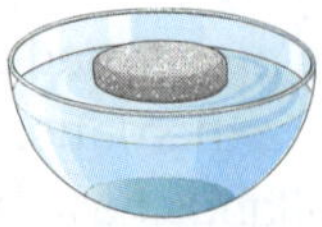

Science in Context

Additional information on the topic being taught

Science in Context

In a liquid and a gas, the molecules are loosely packed, so they have some regions with more molecules and other regions with fewer molecules. The movement f molecules from a region igher concentration t ... lower con...

Challenge Yourself

Questions testing students' ability to reason and extrapolate

Challenge Yourself

You might have noticed that cut pieces of some vegetables and fruits like potato, apple, etc., turn brown when exposed to air if they are not consumed immediately. you know what kind of a ... it is?

Know the Scientist

Famous scientists and their contribution to the topic at hand

Know the Scientist

Joseph Priestley (1733–1804) was an English chemist. He is credited for the isolation and discovery of oxygen in its gaseous state. He named it as 'dephlogisticated air'. He also synthesized nitrous oxide (laughing gas).

Activity 1

Aim: To study that matter has mass

Materials required: Two paper bags, some marbles and a weighing balance

Procedure:

1. Weigh the two empty paper bags using a weighing balance.
2. Now add some marbles to one of the paper bags.

Observation: The paper bag that is fille
arbles becomes heavier when com
mpty one.

Activity

To hone experimental and deduction skills

Revision Zone

In-text questions for assessing progress

Revision Zone

Give one word for each of the following.

1. The substance formed when two or mo atoms are bound together ______
2. The pure substance that contains only kind of atoms ______
3. The number of atoms present in a mol of an element ______
4. The chemical formula of ammonia ______

Keywords

Pure substance: a substance that consists of only one kir

Mixture: a substance that contains two or more different

Winnowing: a method that uses the action of wind to sepa a mixture

Sieving: a method that uses a sieve to separate undesirabl

Filtration: the process of using a porous medium (filter) to s particles suspended in a liquid

Distillation: the method of separation of components of and condensation

Centrifugation: the process of separation of fine, inso using a centrifuge

ctional distillation: the process of separation ference in their boiling points

Keywords

Definitions of key terms from the chapter

ose the odd one out. Give reasons for the choice.

a. Carbon, gold, copper, aluminium
b. Chlorine, sulphur, germanium, iodine
c. Silver, water, zinc, calcium
d. O, C, Au, Mg
e. N, ZnO, H, Cd

7 **Differentiate between the following.**

a. Melting and freezing
b. Vaporization and condensation
c. Elements and compounds
d. Metals and non-metals
e. An atom and a molecule

8 **Give reasons for the following.**

Solids are hard and rigid.
ids take the shape of

Exercise

Variety of questions given at the end of each chapter

Worksheet

Subject Integration

Identify the preservative methods that are suitable for the food items given below.

Food item	Preservation method used	Reason for selecting the metho
Milk 		
Fish 		
Pulses 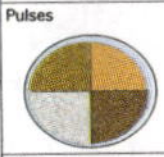		
Meat 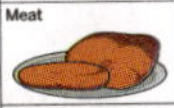		
Fruits 		

Worksheet

Thematic worksheets on integration of knowledge across subjects and Life Skills

Contents

Introduction to Chemistry

1

Introduction

What I shall learn

- What is chemistry?
- Development of chemistry
- Importance of chemistry in daily life
- Use of chemistry in various fields

Science plays an important role in the life of human beings. The application of science has helped us to invent different types of machines, and mediums of communication and transport. The greatest contributions of science have been in the field of medicine. The computer is yet another important invention of science. All these innovative developments have made our everyday life easier, more comfortable and more progressive than it was in ancient times. Thus, science affects our daily life in all possible ways.

The word 'science' is derived from the Latin word *scientia*, which means 'knowledge'. Science can be divided into three main branches: physics, chemistry and biology.

- Physics deals with the study of natural phenomena and the effects of various forces in nature.
- Chemistry deals with the study of the properties and composition of substances.
- Biology deals with the study of living things.

All the three branches of science are interrelated.

What is Chemistry?

Chemistry is the branch of science that deals with the study of the composition, structure, properties and reactions of substances. The word 'chemistry' is derived from the word 'alchemy'.

Chemistry requires a lot of experimentation. An **experiment** is a scientific test carried out to study what happens when certain conditions are fulfilled, find the cause of something, discover new things and gain new knowledge. In chemistry, experiments are conducted to discover new compounds or find out new methods that would lead to the creation of new compounds. During experimentation, we study the properties and composition of compounds along with their reactions with other substances.

A scientist's discoveries have to be submitted to the scientific community in order to be accepted as a new invention. These discoveries are made in the form of a theory that has several steps. Now, let us learn how the field of chemistry has developed.

Do You Know?

A **scientist** is a person who specializes in any branch of science and conducts experiments in that particular field to make new discoveries. A person who studies chemistry is called a **chemist**.

Development of Chemistry

Ancient Greeks believed the existence of only four elements: water, earth, air and fire. The Greek philosopher Aristotle believed that matter is made up of these four elements and has the properties of coldness, hotness, wetness and dryness.

Influenced by Aristotle's ideas, during 300 BC–300 AD, alchemists intended to find various ways that can transform the cheaper metals into gold. They used a substance for this conversion called 'Philospher's stone'. Alchemists were also interested in finding the chemical composition that would make people live longer and cure diseases. But they were not successful.

Even though alchemists' approach towards chemistry was not systematic but they made significant contributions to the field of chemistry that includes the 'discovery of mercury (quicksilver)' and the 'preparation of various strong acids'. During sixteenth century, the extraction of metals from ores and other major contributions were made in *'metallurgy'*.

The iron pillar situated near Qutub Minar in New Delhi, is a classic example for the metallurgical skills that existed in the olden days. This pillar is made of pure iron. Scientists firmly say that it is very difficult to produce such pure iron even in small quantities using electrolysis process.

By looking at the historical evidences, we can summarize that there was an existence of knowledge in the fields of metallurgy and metalworking in the olden days. This paved way for the preparation of alloys and extraction of metals in recent times.

Know the Scientist

John Dalton (1766–1844) was the first scientist to use symbols to represent elements. He was an English chemist, who postulated the atomic theory. He was the first person to explain the difference between an atom and a molecule. His theory supports the law of conservation of mass.

Importance of Chemistry in Daily Life

The most amazing fact about chemistry is that it is an integral part of our life. Every component of our surroundings, such as the water we drink, the air we inhale and exhale, the food we consume and most of the substances that we use in our daily life involve various chemical substances and chemical processes. In fact, the human body is also made up of chemical substances like sodium, calcium, iron, minerals and vitamins.

- Water, which constitutes about 70 per cent of the human body, is made up of two chemical substances: hydrogen and oxygen.
- Air is a mixture of gases like carbon dioxide, oxygen, nitrogen and argon.
- Soaps, liquid cleaners and detergents are made of chemicals like sodium carbonate and potassium carbonate.

Know the Scientist

Marie Curie was a French chemist born in 1867. She discovered a radioactive material called **radium**. Radium is used in the treatment of cancer. She was the first woman to win a Nobel Prize.

- The food that we consume is made up of a variety of compounds. Carbohydrates, proteins and fats are chemical substances present in our food.

Activity 1

Aim: To make a list of products used in daily life since morning.

Procedure: We use many products since morning such as toothpaste, soap, shampoo, cream, pencil, rubber, etc. Make a note of items that you use daily.

____

____

____

Observation and discussion: Discuss with teacher and students about the origin of these products. Are these products applications of chemistry?

Use of Chemistry in Various Fields

Let us look at how chemistry is used in various industries and fields.

Challenge Yourself

Antiseptics and disinfectants are both chemical substances that hinder the growth of harmful microorganisms. We apply only antiseptics on our body to prevent infections in wounds but do not apply disinfectants. Why?

Food and Chemistry

Chemistry has a great impact on our everyday life. Chemicals derived directly from the natural sources or synthetically obtained help us in preserving food items from spoilage and to increase their shelf life. They also help us to analyse the nutrients present in the food for our better use and to develop novel or improved varieties of food.

Food Preservation: Preservation of food is the process of preventing the spoilage of different food items that need to be stored for long periods. It includes retaining their colour, taste and nutritive value.

Food Processing: Food processing is the conversion of raw ingredients by either physical or chemical means into food. These food items are usually packed in cans or boxes. Some methods that are used for the processing of food are canning, pickling, pasteurization, fermentation, freezing and refrigeration, irradiation and dehydration.

Soft drinks, cheese, bread, milk, tinned vegetables and meat products are few examples of processed food.

Advantages of food preservation:

Food preservation helps us in the following ways:

1. To prevent ourselves from falling sick due to consumption of contaminated food.
2. To take care of the excess food produced or grown.
3. To add variety in food by making different fruits and vegetables available during off season.

4. To lengthen the shelf life of food by slowing down the spoilage of food caused by microorganisms.
5. To transport food to areas where it is not grown.
6. To make transportation and storage of food easier.
7. To supply food to hospitals, airlines, trains, defence personnel and astronauts.

Some techniques used for food preservation are as follows:

- **Sun drying:** The moisture content in food is removed by drying it in the sun. The absence of moisture prevents the multiplication of microorganisms. Most of the cereals, pulses and spices are stored by this method.
- **Heating:** Boiling of water is the basic cooking practice to prevent the spread of diseases due to microorganisms. The same technique is used to store milk. A new technique called the ultra-heat treatment is used to store milk, wherein the milk is heated to 135° C for a few seconds and stored in tetra-packs.
- **Salting:** Fish is the main food that is stored using salt. Moisture is absorbed by the salt, keeping the fish dry.
- **Sugaring:** Jams, jellies and fruit squashes are stored using sugar content. Sugar inhibits the growth of microorganisms by drawing out water from their cells. *Jamoon* is preserved for long periods using sugar syrup.
- **Using oil and vinegar:** Pickles, fish, fruits and meat are preserved in oil and vinegar.
- **Pasteurization:** This is a technique used to store milk. Milk is heated to about 70° C for 30 minutes and cooled quickly. This kills the microorganisms and does not affect the flavour of the milk due to heating.
- **Freezing:** Refrigerators are used in all households, restaurants and warehouses for storing vegetables and other food items. The temperature in these is maintained at 5° C. This prevents the growth of microorganisms on the food. Deep freezing is used to store food for a longer duration (for months) at temperatures below –18° C.
- **Canning:** After the heating or sterilization of food, it is stored in airtight containers to prevent contamination due to microorganisms.
- **Using chemical preservatives:** Chemicals like sodium benzoate and sodium metabisulphate are used to store jams, ketchups, fruit juices, etc. Sodium nitrite, sulphur dioxide, sodium sorbate and potassium sorbate are a few other chemical preservatives used for food preservation.

Everyday Science

Onions release a gas called propanethial S-oxide that causes burning sensation in our eyes. Hence, we 'cry' while cutting an onion.

Know the Scientist

Dmitri Ivanovich Mendeleev (1834–1907) was a Russian chemist. He is popularly known as the 'Father of the Periodic Table'. Mendeleev not only explained about the organization of elements in the periodic table, but also was the first person to use his periodic table to predict the existence of eight new elements and their properties. On recognition of his contributions, the element 101 is named as *Mendelevium*.

Revision Zone

State whether the following statements are true or false.

1. An experiment may be conducted to find the cause of something.
2. Fruits and vegetables do not contain chemical compounds.
3. Sugar inhibits the growth of microorganisms.
4. Processed foods have shorter shelf life.
5. Sodium metabisulphite is a chemical preservative.

Cosmetics and Chemistry

Cosmetics are the substances that are used to improve the appearance or odour of the human body. These substances are mostly a mixture of chemical compounds which are derived either naturally or synthetically.

Chemistry and cosmetology are closely related to each other. All the beauty products that we predominantly use like creams, lotions, shampoos, shaving creams, serums, lipsticks and nail polish are synthesized from combinations of various chemicals. For instance, when people dye their hair, the colour change caused is due to the result of a chemical reaction that takes place.

Composition of few cosmetics is given below:

▲ Cosmetic products

Talcum Powder: Talcum powder is obtained from a mineral known as *'talc'.* It is composed of elements like magnesium, oxygen and silicon. It is popularly used in cosmetic products mainly as body and facial powder to protect against the dirt and keep the skin dry.

Cream and body lotion: Creams and body lotions are used mainly to moisturize the skin and prevent it from drying, especially in the winter season. Various ingredients are used in these products which include glycerin, seed oils, aloe vera, vitamin E, scents, synthetic colours and several chemical substances.

Clothing and Chemistry

In textiles, a lot of chemicals are used in the form of dyes, mordants and bleaches. Nylon, polyester and rayon are synthetic fibres used to make cloth. These fibres are made using chemical processes. Flax, cotton and wool were the earliest natural fibres used by humans for clothing. With more and more research in chemistry, scientists have developed synthetic fibres which are more durable, wrinkle-resistant and dry easily. Terycot is an example of blended fabric made from polyester and cotton. It has high absorbing quality of cotton as well as wrinkle-resistance of polyester.

▲ Sarees

Chemicals in Industries

Cleansing agents are the substances that are used for the purpose of removing stains or impurities or dirt or bad odour. These substances are used in either liquid or granule or powder or spray form. The selection of cleansing agents for the removal of stains depends on the following factors:

- composition of the cleaning agents
- type of stain/impurity/dirt to be removed
- type of surface to be cleaned
- effectiveness of cost, time and effort
- hazardous effects of cleaning agents

▲ Cleansing action of soaps and detergents

Some common types of cleansing agents used are given below.

a. **Soaps and detergents:** They are cleansing agents used for washing and cleaning processes. Soaps are sodium or potassium salts of long chain fatty acids. They are manufactured by the saponification of oils and fats. **Saponification** is the process in which sodium hydroxide reacts with oils or fats and breaks them down to form salts of respective fatty acids. Soaps are generally prepared as solid cakes. Perfumes and colours are added to soaps before casting and drying them into cakes.

Detergents are made from petroleum products. Alkyl benzene is the main raw material used to manufacture detergents. Detergents are generally prepared in powdered form. They have a better cleansing action than soaps because detergents produce more lather, even in hard water. Soaps, on the other hand, form an insoluble precipitate called **scum** with hard water, which sticks to clothes, making them look unclean. A disadvantage of detergents is that they are not biodegradable and cause water pollution.

Cleansing action of soaps and detergents: The molecules of soap or detergent have two parts: a **hydrophobic** part, which means water repellant, and a **hydrophilic** part, which means attracted to water.

When soap or detergent is applied to dirty clothes soaked in water, the hydrophobic part attaches to the dirt molecules and the hydrophilic part attaches to the water molecules. When there is movement of water, the hydrophilic part moves along with the water and thus pulls the hydrophobic part too that is attached to the dirt particles. In this way, dirt is removed from the clothes.

b. **Alkaline-based cleaning agents:** These are extensively used for removing the stains caused due to grease in laundry. A few examples are washing soda (sodium carbonate), caustic soda (sodium hydroxide) and bleach (sodium hypochlorite).

c. **Acid-based cleaning agents:** These are extensively used in the industries for metal cleaning and in the removal of stains from hard floors. A few examples are dilute hydrochloric acid, citric acid, acetic acid and oxalic acid.

d. **Disinfectants:** These are extensively used to kill harmful bacteria. A few examples are chlorine, iodine and phenol.

e. **Solvent cleaners:** These are mainly used in the dry cleaning for removal of stains and in the cleaning of mirrors and windows. A few examples are acetone, turpentine and methylated spirits.

Chemicals as Medicines

Chemistry plays an important role in the medical field. With the knowledge of chemistry, many medicines have been prepared for the treatment and prevention of various diseases. Medicines are chemical substances that can be either obtained naturally (from plants or animals) or prepared from chemicals. They can be of different types depending on the type of illness to be cured and their nature of action. Some commonly used medicines are as follows:

- **Analgesics**: They are pain killers because they provide relief from pain. Aspirin, paracetamol and naproxen are the commonly used analgesics. Aspirin is chemically known as 'acetylsalicylic acid'. It is used as a pain killer to give relief from pain or fever. It is also used to reduce the swelling caused due to arthritis. Paracetamol is chemically known as 'acetaminophen'. It is commonly used in the treatment of fever, pain, headache and arthritis. Taking more dosage of Paracetamol than the required amount may lead to the damage of the liver.
- **Antacids**: They are used to reduce acidity in the stomach caused by production of extra gastric acid (HCl). These give relief from burning sensation or stomach pain. Milk of magnesia is commonly used as it is an alkali and neutralizes the acidity of the stomach.
- **Antipyretics**: They are used to reduce fever and pain. Paracetamol and aspirin are also used as antipyretics.
- **Antibiotics**: They are used to treat infections caused by microorganisms. Antibiotics are chemicals extracted from microorganisms to kill or prevent the growth of other disease-causing microorganisms. Penicillin, streptomycin and tetracycline are commonly used antibiotics.
- **Antiseptics**: They are applied on cuts, boils, wounds, bruises or burns to prevent the growth of microorganisms. Commonly used antiseptics are Dettol, hydrogen peroxide and tincture of iodine.

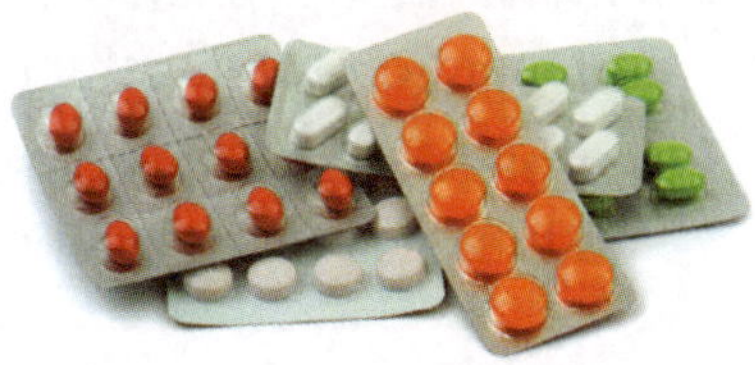

▲ Medicines

- **Antihistamines**: They are used to prevent or treat allergy. Some people are allergic to dust or particular foods like brinjal and sea food. They develop rashes, fever, sneezing or breathlessness when an allergic reaction takes place in their body. To treat such cases, antihistamines are used. Diphenhydramine (Benadryl) and Cetirizine (Zyrtec) are commonly used antihistamines.

Plants also contain chemicals that can be used to prevent or cure diseases. For instance, the parts of a neem tree (bark, fruits and leaves) have antiseptic properties and are used to treat skin infections. *Tulsi* has antipyretic properties. Mint leaves are used as antacids to relieve stomach ache and heartburn. The gel in the leaves of *Aloe vera* plant is used for quick healing of skin conditions like wounds and burns. Its sap acts as a strong laxative. Ginger can be used to treat motion sickness. Juice of bitter gourd is highly beneficial for diabetic patients.

Know the Scientist

Antoine Laurent de Lavoisier (1743–1794) was a French chemist. He is popularly known as the 'Father of modern chemistry'. He gave the names for the elements hydrogen, carbon and oxygen. He discovered the role of oxygen in the process of combustion and respiration. Lavoisier was the first person to explain the principle of mass conservation. He is considered as one of the great contributors to the chemical revolution and for the reform of the chemical nomenclature.

Science in Context

The iron pillar near Qutab Minar, Delhi is a 24-feet high pillar that draws the attention of scientists across the world. Made of a unique composition of metals, it is considered a marvel that has withstood rusting for many decades.

(a) *Tulsi* plant

(b) Neem tree

▲ Medicinal plants

Revision Zone

Fill in the blanks.

1. When a dirty shirt is soaked in soap water, the hydrophobic part attaches to the __________ molecules.
2. The disadvantage of detergents is that they are __________.
3. Analgesics are used to reduce __________ .
4. __________ are medicines used to prevent or treat allergy.

Keywords

Chemistry: the branch of science that deals with the study of composition, structure, properties, and reactions of substances

Experiment: a scientific test done to study what happens when certain conditions are fulfilled, find the cause of something, discover new things and gain new knowledge

In a Nutshell

- The three main branches of science are physics, chemistry and biology.
- Chemistry is the branch of science that deals with the composition, properties and reactions of substances.
- Chemistry has applications in various fields like medicine, food, clothing, cosmetics and industries.

Exercise

1 Choose the correct answer for each of the following.

a. Which of the following branches of science deals with the study of living things?

i. Chemistry ii. Biology
iii. Physics iv. Geology

b. Which of the following scientists first explained the difference between an atom and a molecule?

i. Lavoisier ii. John Dalton
iii. Mendeleev iv. Einstein

c. Which of the following is an alkaline based cleaning agent?

i. Caustic soda ii. Iodine
iii. Acetone iv. Citric acid

d. Which of the following is extensively used to kill harmful bacteria?

i. Chlorine ii. Turpentine
iii. Citric acid iv. Acetic acid

e. The main raw material used in the manufacture of detergents is

i. Oil ii. Alkyl benzene
iii. Citric acid iv. Phenol

f. Identify the antiseptic among the following.

i. Penicillin
ii. Hydrogen peroxide
iii. Benadryl iv. Aspirin

2 Fill in the blanks.

a. Milk can be preserved by ______________ (pasteurization/salting) technique.

b. Soaps are manufactured by the process of __________ (polymerization/saponification) of oils and fats.

c. The branch of science that deals with the study of the properties and composition of substances is ____________.(physics/chemistry)

d. The name of the elements oxygen and hydrogen is given by the scientist _________ (Dalton/Lavoisier).

e. Sodium benzoate is an example of _________ (laxative/preservative).

f. Dehydration is a method used in the _________ (clothing/food) industry.

3 Write T for True and F for False.

a. The element 101 is named as '*Mendelevium*' for the contributions made by the scientist Mendeleev.

b. Sodium metabisulphate is a chemical used to preserve ketchups.

c. Glycerin and scents are used in the manufacture of lotions.

d. Cotton is not mixed with other synthetic fibres in the creation of fabrics.

e. Acetylsalicylic acid is the other name of Paracetamol.

4 Choose the odd one out. Give reasons for the choice.

a. Chlorine, citric acid, iodine, phenol

b. Washing soda, bleach, turpentine, caustic soda

c. Methylated spirits, bleach, acetone, turpentine

d. Talc, Paracetamol, Aspirin; Penicillin

e. Shampoos, lipsticks, phenol, talc

5 Define the following terms.

a. Cleansing agents

b. Food preservation

c. Food processing

d. Cosmetics

e. Antacids

f. Antipyretics

6 Give reasons for the following.

a. Use of sugar and salt as preserving agents.

b. Detergents have a better cleansing action than soaps.

c. More dosage of paracetamol should be avoided.

d. Use of pasteurization to preserve the milk.

7 Answer the following questions in brief.

a. Distinguish between soaps and detergents.

b. Write the composition of the chemicals in talcum powder.

c. Mention few examples of food preservatives.

d. Write the methods used for the processing of food.

e. Mention the role of paracetamol in medicines.

f. What is the difference between antipyretics and antibiotics?

g. What kind of medicinal properties do plants have?

8 Answer the following questions in detail.

a. Write a note on the development of chemistry from historical perspective.

b. Describe the use of chemicals in the field of cosmetics.

c. Explain the role of chemicals as medicines.

d. Explain the cleansing action of soaps and detergents.

9 Think and answer.

Medicines and cosmetics come with an expiry date. Can you tell why? What is the significance of manufacturing date and expiry date marked on such products?

10 Project

Organize a visit to a chemical industry (dye, plastic, fertilizer, detergents or drugs) under strict supervision. Ask students to observe the raw materials, machines and processes used there. The students should prepare a report based on the visit and submit it to the teacher.

11 In the Library

The different branches of chemistry are organic chemistry, inorganic chemistry, biochemistry, physical chemistry and analytical chemistry. Find what each of these branches deal with and what are their applications.

Worksheet

Subject Integration

Identify the preservative methods that are suitable for the food items given below.

Food item	Preservation method used	Reason for selecting the method
Milk 		
Fish 		
Pulses 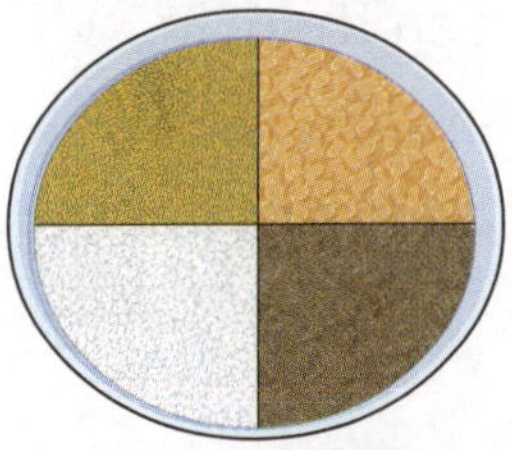		
Meat 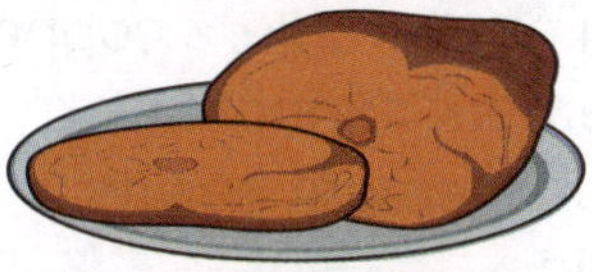		
Fruits 		
Jam and jelly 		

Elements, Compounds and Mixtures

2

Introduction

What I shall learn

- Element
- Compound
- Mixture
- Methods of separating mixtures

We come across different types of substances in our daily life. These substances come in different forms and combinations. So, based on their composition, substances can be classified as pure and mixed substances. Generally, a substance is considered to be pure if it is clean or free from impurities. But scientifically, a pure substance is a substance that consists of only one kind of atoms or molecules. Most of the substances found in nature are impure or mixed substances. For example, the air we breathe is a mixture of different gases and the water we drink contains many minerals. Let us learn about pure and mixed substances, and the differences between them in this chapter.

A substance that consists of only one kind of atoms or molecules is called a **pure substance**. There are two types of pure substances: elements and compounds.

Element

An **element** is a pure substance that consists of only one kind of atoms. For example, a copper vessel made from the element copper has only copper atoms in it. An element cannot be broken down into simpler substances either physically or chemically. Each element has its own individual properties. Examples are gold, copper, iron, calcium and zinc.

Characteristic features of elements are as follows:

(a) Gold (element) (b) Salt (compound)

▲ Pure substances

- Elements consist of only one kind of atoms. In other words, an element is made up of identical atoms.
- Each element has its own unique, individual properties.
- The atoms of an element show the same properties as the element.
- Elements cannot be separated or broken down into simpler components by physical or chemical methods.

Classification of Elements

All the elements in nature differ from each other in their properties. Elements are divided into two broad classes—metals and non-metals—based on the following properties:

- **Malleability**: the ability of a substance to be beaten into thin sheets
- **Brittleness**: the ability of a substance to be broken into pieces
- **Ductility**: the ability of a substance to be stretched into thin wires
- **Conductivity**: the ability of a substance to allow heat and electricity to pass through it
  It is of two types:
  Thermal conductivity: the ability of a substance to allow heat to pass through it
  Electrical conductivity: the ability of a substance to allow electricity to pass through it
- **Sonority**: the ability of a substance to produce a ringing sound when struck with a hard object

The properties of metals and non-metals are summarized in Table 2.1.

Table 2.1 Properties of metals and non-metals

Metals	Non-metals
Metals are mostly solids at room temperature.	Non-metals exist in solid or gaseous state at room temperature.
Metals have a shiny surface, i.e., they have lustre. Thus, some metals are used to make ornaments.	Non-metals are not shiny in appearance, i.e., they lack lustre.
Metals are hard.	Non-metals are soft.
Most of the metals are malleable.	Non-metals are not malleable.
Metals are not brittle.	Non-metals are brittle.
Most of the metals are ductile.	Non-metals are non-ductile.
Most metals are good conductors of heat. Hence, they are widely used to make cooking utensils.	Most non-metals are bad conductors of heat.
Most metals are good conductors of electricity. Hence, they are widely used to make wires and electrical appliances.	Most non-metals are bad conductors of electricity.
Most metals are sonorous. Hence, they are used to make objects like bells.	Non-metals are non-sonorous.
Examples: Sodium, copper, gold, iron, aluminium	Examples: Carbon, oxygen, sulphur, chlorine, iodine

Metalloids

Some elements show the properties of both metals and non-metals. Such elements are called **metalloids**. Metalloids have a metallic appearance. They are brittle and fair conductors of electricity. They are used in the manufacturing of glass and semiconducting devices. Boron, silicon, germanium, arsenic, antimony and tellurium are a few examples of metalloids.

Use of Symbols to Represent Elements

So far, about 118 elements have been discovered. The short forms or abbreviations used to denote the names of elements are known as **chemical symbols**. In earlier times, pictorial representations of the elements were used. Later, letters representing the names of the elements began to be used as symbols. All these names and symbols are approved by the International Union of Pure and Applied Chemistry (IUPAC). The features of the modern method of representation of symbols are given below:

1. The first letter of the name of the element, usually written in capitals, is used as the symbol. For example, C for carbon, O for oxygen and N for nitrogen.
2. If two or more elements have their names starting with the same letter, then a two-letter symbol is used. The first letter of the name is the first letter of the symbol and the next non-repeating letter of the name is the second letter of the symbol. The first letter is written in capitals and the second letter in small. For example, C for carbon, Ca for calcium, Cd for cadmium, Cl for chlorine, Co for cobalt and Pt for platinum.
3. For a few elements, the symbols are taken from their Latin names. For example, the Latin name of potassium is *kalium* and hence K is used as its symbol. Similarly, the Latin name of gold is *aurum* and its symbol is Au.

Tables 2.2 and 2.3 give the symbols of some elements.

Table 2.2 First 20 elements and their symbols

Element	Symbol
Hydrogen	H
Helium	He
Lithium	Li
Beryllium	Be
Boron	B
Carbon	C
Nitrogen	N
Oxygen	O
Fluorine	F
Neon	Ne
Sodium	Na
Magnesium	Mg
Aluminium	Al
Silicon	Si
Phosphorus	P
Sulphur	S
Chlorine	Cl
Argon	Ar
Potassium	K
Calcium	Ca

Table 2.3 Some elements with their Latin names and symbols

Element	Latin name	Symbol
Sodium	*Natrium*	Na
Potassium	*Kalium*	K
Gold	*Aurum*	Au
Silver	*Argentum*	Ag
Iron	*Ferrum*	Fe

Compound

A **compound** is a pure substance formed when two or more elements combine together in a fixed ratio. It is made up of the same kind of molecules. In other words, when two or more elements react chemically, the elements lose their original properties and a compound with new properties is formed.

For example, carbon dioxide is made up of one atom of carbon and two atoms of oxygen. The properties of carbon dioxide are very different from that of a carbon atom or an oxygen atom. Carbon is a solid but carbon dioxide is a gas.

Other examples of compounds are water, salt and sugar.

Activity 1

Aim: To explain the formation of iron sulphide (FeS) from iron (Fe) and sulphur (S)

Materials required: Glass test tube, iron filings, sulphur, weighing balance, spatula, test tube holder and Bunsen burner

Procedure:

1. Weigh 3 g of iron filings and 3 g of sulphur separately with the help of a weighing balance.
2. Transfer these contents carefully into a clean glass test tube.
3. Carefully heat this mixture using a Bunsen burner and observe what happens.

Observation: The reaction between sulphur and iron filings takes place very quickly. As the sulphur melts, it reacts with iron and results in the formation a new compound called iron sulphide.

$$\text{Fe (Iron)} + \text{S (Sulphur)} \longrightarrow \text{FeS (Iron sulphide)}$$

This reaction is an exothermic reaction. The heat that is produced during this reaction vaporizes sulphur and gradually the sulphur vapours burn with a light blue-coloured flame.

Challenge Yourself

We have learned about the individual characteristics of both elements and compounds. Keeping them in mind, write the general characteristics of pure substances.

Characteristic features of compounds are as follows:

- Compounds are formed when two or more elements combine chemically in a fixed ratio.
- The properties of compounds are different from the properties of their constituent elements.
- Compounds exhibit their own physical and chemical properties.
- Compounds can be separated into their individual components by chemical methods.

Molecule

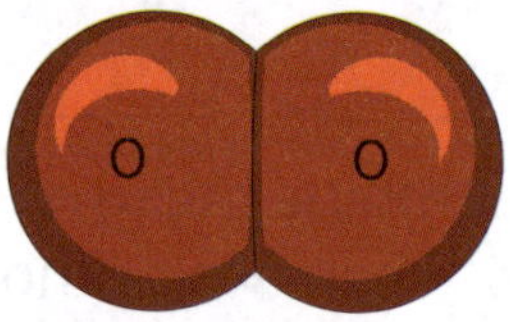

▲ Oxygen molecule (molecule of an element)

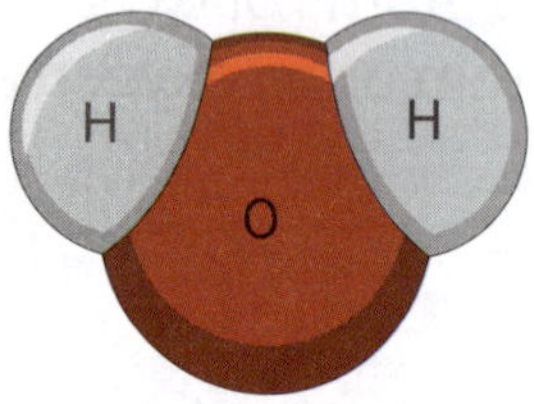

▲ Water molecule (molecule of a compound)

When two or more atoms of the same element or different elements combine, they form a molecule. The combining atoms are chemically bound or joined together to form molecule. A **molecule** can be defined as the smallest particle of an element or a compound that exhibits all the properties of that element or compound and can exist independently. Depending on whether a molecule is formed from atoms of the same element or different elements, molecules are of two types: molecule of an element and molecule of a compound.

- When two or more atoms of the same element combine, a **molecule of an element** is formed. In molecules like oxygen (O_2), hydrogen (H_2), nitrogen (N_2) and chlorine (Cl_2), the same kind of atoms or atoms of the same element are bound together to form a molecule.
- When two or more atoms of different elements combine in a fixed proportion, a **molecule of a compound** is formed. In molecules like water (H_2O), calcium oxide (CaO), zinc chloride ($ZnCl_2$) and carbon dioxide (CO_2), different kinds of atoms or atoms of different elements are bound together to form a molecule.

Revision Zone

Give one word for each of the following.

1. The pure substance that contains only one kind of atoms ________
2. Elements that show the properties of both metals and non-metals ________
3. The abbreviations used to denote the names of elements ________
4. The substance formed when two or more elements are chemically bound together ________

Mixture

A **mixture** is a substance that contains two or more different substances (elements, compounds or both) mixed together in such a way that no chemical change occurs between them. The different types of substances present in a mixture are called its **components** or

constituents. Air, tap water, oil in water, sugar in water, soil and alloys are a few examples of mixtures. In all these mixtures, the concentration of the components of the mixture can be different. For example, the concentration of different gases in air varies from place to place and a solution of sugar can be prepared by adding variable amounts of sugar to water. Characteristic features of mixtures are as follows:

▲ Mixture of pulses

- A mixture does not exhibit any characteristic property of its own. The components of a mixture do not lose their properties and thus retain their original properties in the mixture.
- In a mixture, the components are not present in any fixed ratio or proportion.
- The components of a mixture can be separated easily through physical methods of separation.
- Mixtures are not pure substances as they contain more than one type of component.

Table 2.4 gives the comparison between compounds and mixtures.

Table 2.4 Comparison between compounds and mixtures

Compounds	Mixtures
A compound is made up of two or more elements mixed together chemically.	A mixture is made up of two or more substances that are not mixed together chemically.
Compounds exhibit new properties. They do not show the properties of their constituent elements.	Mixtures do not exhibit new properties. They retain the same properties of their individual components.
The ratio of components in a compound is fixed.	The ratio of components in a mixture is not fixed.
The components of a compound cannot be separated by physical methods.	The components of a mixture can be separated by physical methods.
Compounds are pure substances.	Mixtures are impure substances.

Separation of Mixtures

We know that a mixture is not a pure substance. It consists of different types of components. Of these components, some may be useful and some may not be of use. To use only the desirable components, separation is required. Separation of mixtures is necessary due to the following reasons:

- To separate useful components from a mixture. For example, by churning milk, cream is separated from milk so that both the components can be used appropriately.
- To remove unwanted materials or impurities from a mixture. For example, separation of husk from rice grains, unwanted stones from rice grains or pulses before cooking and separation of unwanted leaves from raw leafy vegetables.
- To get desirable or pure substances. For example, in preparation of tea, tea leaves are separated from brewed tea.

Methods of Separating Mixtures

▲ Sieving

Different components of a mixture have different chemical and physical properties. Hence, selecting the appropriate method of separation for a mixture depends on the characteristic properties of each component. Let us learn about a few separation techniques of mixtures into their components in the following sections.

Sieving: The method of using a sieve to separate undesirable components from a mixture is called **sieving**. This method of separation is based on the difference in the sizes of the components to be separated. When using a sieve, the following steps are followed:

1. The mixture to be sieved is taken in a sieve.
2. A bowl is kept under the sieve and the sieve is shaken to and fro.
3. The larger component is left behind in the sieve, while the smaller component passes through the pores of the sieve and collects in the bowl.

According to the size and kind of component to be separated, sieves with different pore sizes are available for use. For example, sieves with fine pores are used to remove bran from wheat flour before making dough. At construction sites, sieves with large pores are used to separate stones and pebbles from sand.

Activity 2

Aim: To separate a mixture using the sieving process

Materials required: A mixture of talcum powder, raisins and black pepper, sieves with different pore sizes and a bowl

Procedure:

1. Take the mixture in a sieve with a small pore size.
2. Place a bowl below the sieve and shake the sieve to and fro.
3. Now, take the larger components that were left behind in the sieve.
4. Take a sieve with a pore size larger than that of the previous sieve.
5. Add the components and shake to and fro.
6. Now, much larger components are left behind in the sieve.

Observation: When the mixture is passed through a sieve with a small pore size, the talcum powder separates first, leaving behind black pepper and raisins. Then, when the remaining components of the mixture are passed through a sieve with a larger pore size (which is enough for black pepper to pass through), the black pepper separates from the mixture, leaving behind only raisins in the sieve. Thus, all the three components of the mixture are separated using the sieving process.

Science in Context

The outlet pipes of industries are fitted with magnets to remove toxic iron and iron oxide components from the waste products before they are let into water bodies.

Magnetic separation: The method of using a magnet to separate magnetic components from a mixture is called **magnetic separation**. This method is based on the difference in the magnetic properties of the components to be separated, that is, a magnetic substance gets attracted to a magnet. In this method, a magnet is rotated over a mixture so that the magnetic components cling to the magnet, while the nonmagnetic components are left behind.

Activity 3

Aim: To separate a mixture of sand and iron filings using the magnetic separation method

Materials required: Iron filings, sand, bowls and a magnet

Procedure:

1. Make a mixture of sand and iron filings.
2. Place the mixture in a bowl.
3. Now, hover a magnet over the mixture and rotate it over the mixture. What do you see?

Observation: The iron filings get attracted and cling to the magnet leaving behind the sand.

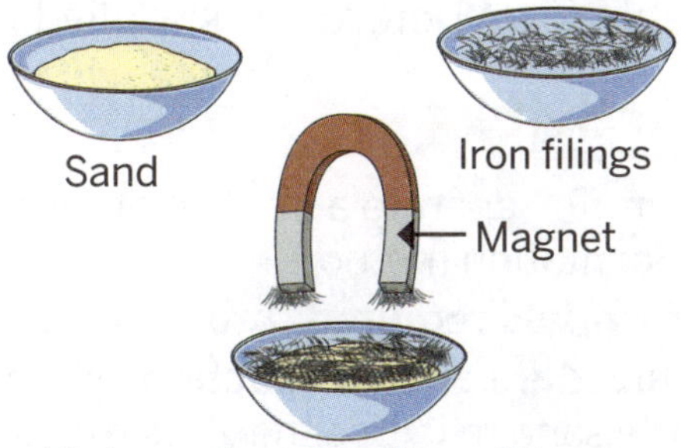

This method is used in industries to remove scrap iron from a garbage heap with the help of a large magnet fitted to a crane.

Sublimation: The process in which a solid changes directly into its gaseous state without passing through its liquid state is called **sublimation**. This method is used when a mixture contains a component that can sublime. The set-up for sublimation is shown in the figure given alongside.

In this method, the mixture is taken in an evaporating dish. When the mixture is heated, the solid component that sublimes evaporates as vapours, leaving behind the component that does not sublime in the dish. Then, the sublimed solid is obtained by cooling the vapours. Thus, the mixture is separated.

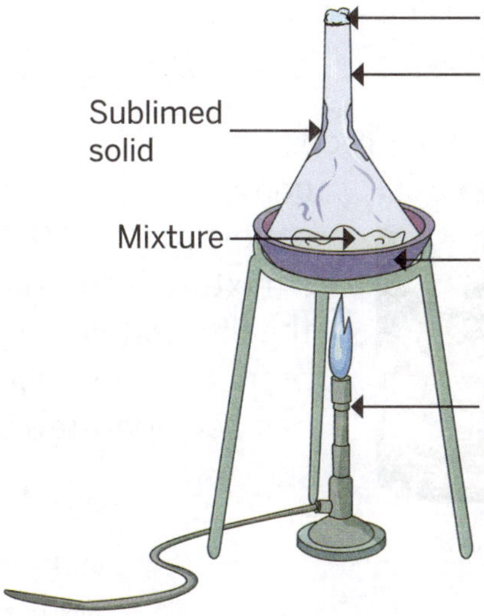

▲ Sublimation

Iodine, camphor, naphthalene and ammonium chloride are sublimable substances.

Sedimentation and decantation: The process of separating insoluble solid components mixed in a liquid by allowing them to settle down at the bottom of the container is called **sedimentation**. This method is based on the difference in the weights of the components of a solid–liquid mixture. In this method, the mixture is kept undisturbed for some time so that the heavier, insoluble solid components settle down at the bottom of the mixture due to the force of gravity. The solid component that settles down during sedimentation is called the **sediment**. The layer of clear liquid on top of the sediment is called the **supernatant liquid**. This clear liquid is then poured out carefully into another container without disturbing the sediment to separate the solid components from the liquid. The process of pouring out the upper layer of clear liquid without disturbing the sediment is called **decantation**.

Science in Context

In water treatment plants, chemicals such as alum are added to make the sedimentation of fine, insoluble solid impurities quicker. Alum sticks to such impurities and forms big lumps. These big lumps being heavier settle down faster. This process is called **loading**.

Sedimentation and decantation methods are used at home while washing pulses in water.

The upper layer of water that contains the impurities is decanted and the sediments (pulses) are retained.

Sedimentation technique is used in water treatment plants to purify water and make it in usable form before it is supplied to our homes.

Activity 4

Aim: To separate a mixture of sand and water using sedimentation and decantation method

Materials required: Two beakers, sand, water and glass rod

Procedure and observation: Fill half of the beaker with water. Add a little sand to it. Use the glass rod to mix the contents. Keep the beaker undisturbed for a few hours. The sand particles settle down at the bottom of the beaker. This happens because the sand particles are heavier than water. A clear layer of water is seen above the settled sand. Without disturbing the sediment of sand, gently pour out the upper layer of water into another beaker. Then the first beaker will be left with the sediment of sand.

Conclusion: Insoluble solid components mixed in a liquid can be separated using sedimentation followed by decantation method.

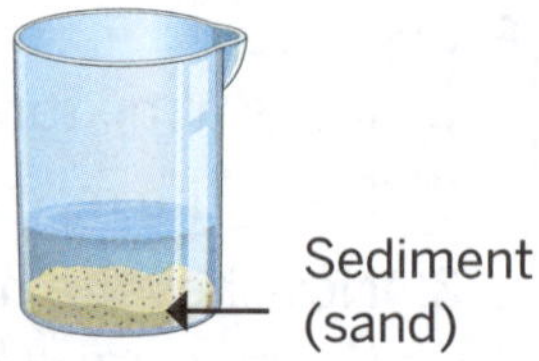

▲ Sedimentation

▲ Decantation

Filtration: The process of using a porous medium (filter) to separate fine, insoluble solid components suspended in a liquid is called **filtration**. Filtration is a simple method that is used to separate mixtures in our daily life. When a mixture is filtered, the fine, insoluble solid components accumulate in the filter, while only the liquid passes through the filter. For instance, while preparing lemon juice, the suspended pulp particles and seeds of lemon can be separated by the filtration method. Likewise, while preparing tea,

▲ Filtration

Activity 5

Aim: To separate a mixture of sand and water using filtration method

Materials required: Two beakers, sand, water, glass rod, filter paper and funnel

Procedure: Add sand and water in a beaker and use the glass rod to mix the contents. Take a filter paper and make a cone by folding it as shown. Place the paper cone in the funnel and keep an empty beaker below the funnel. Gently pour the mixture into the funnel.

Observation: Clear water collects in the beaker after passing through the filter paper and sand particles are left behind in the filter paper.

Conclusion: Filtration is used to separate fine, insoluble solid components suspended in a liquid.

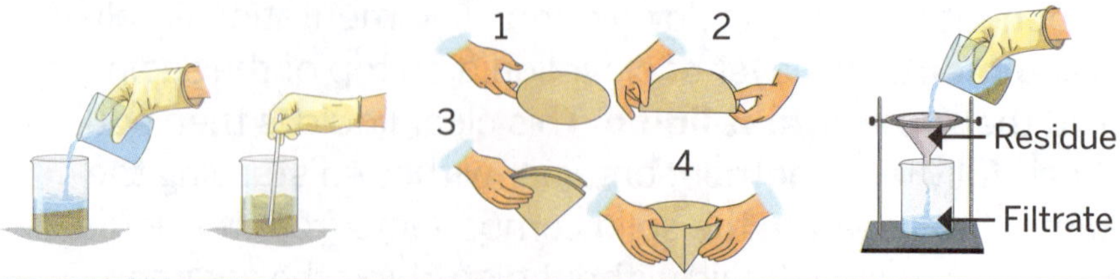

Do You Know?

In earlier times, muslin cloth was used to filter solid–liquid mixtures. Muslin cloth is a thin, porous material made of cotton.

Remember

The insoluble solid component left in the filter is called the **residue**. The liquid passes through the filter is called the **filtrate**.

the unwanted leaves can be removed by filtration.

Filters with different pore sizes are available. The pores of the filter should be smaller than the size of the components that need to be removed.

Evaporation: The process in which a liquid changes into its gaseous state is called **evaporation**. This method involves the evaporation of the liquid component from the mixture while the solid component is left behind. In this method, the liquid component is allowed to evaporate either by heating or by exposing the mixture to sunlight. The evaporated liquid escapes into the atmosphere and thus leaves behind only the solid component.

▲ Separation of salt from sea water by evaporation

Evaporation is used to obtain common salt from sea water. Sea water contains large amounts of salt dissolved in it. It is allowed to flow through narrow channels near coastal areas and is then collected in shallow ponds (called **salt pans**). The water in these salt pans is allowed to dry in the sun. As the water evaporates, solid crystals of salt are left behind. The salt is then collected and sent for purification. The purified salt is used for various purposes.

Activity 6

Aim: To demonstrate the separation of salt from salt solution using evaporation method

Materials required: China dish, salt solution, wire gauze, Bunsen burner and tripod stand

Procedure:

1. Take some salt solution in a China dish.
2. Heat the solution using a Bunsen burner.
3. Boil the solution until the liquid evaporates completely.

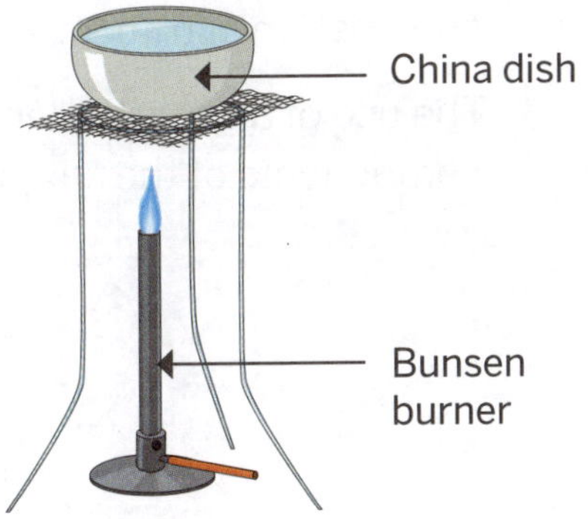

Observation: The solid, white particles of salt are left behind along the inner sides of the China dish after evaporation.

Conclusion: Soluble solids present in a solid–liquid mixture can be separated by evaporation method.

Revision Zone

Write T for True and F for False.

1. The components of a mixture are present in a fixed ratio.
2. At construction sites, sieves with large pores are used.
3. Sublimation method is used when a mixture contains a component that can sublime.
4. Evaporation can be used to separate a mixture of milk and water.

Keywords

Pure substance: a substance that consists of only one kind of atoms or molecules

Element: a pure substance that consists of only one kind of atoms

Chemical symbol: a short form or an abbreviation used to denote the name of elements

Compound: a pure substance formed when two or more elements combine together in a fixed ratio

Mixture: a substance that contains two or more different substances mixed together in such a way that no chemical change occurs between them

Sieving: a method that uses a sieve to separate undesirable components from a mixture. The process of separating insoluble solid components mixed in a liquid by allowing them to settle down at the bottom of the container

Filtration: the process of using a porous medium (filter) to separate fine, insoluble solid components suspended in a liquid

In a Nutshell

- All matter in nature can be broadly classified into pure substances and mixtures.
- Pure substances are of two types: elements and compounds.
- In nature, substances exist mostly in the form of mixtures.
- Mixtures can be separated by using techniques like sieving, sedimentation, decantation, sublimation, filtration, evaporation and magnetic separation.
- The use of any particular separation technique depends upon the properties of the components of the mixture.

Exercise

1 Choose the correct answer for each of the following.

a. A substance that contains two or more substances mixed together without reacting chemically is a ___________.

i. compound ii. mixture
iii. element iv. molecule

b. The ability of a substance to break into pieces is called ___________.

i. malleability ii. ductility
iii. sonority iv. brittleness

c. Which of the following is a property of non-metals?

i. They are solids at room temperature.
ii. They are brittle.
iii. They are malleable.
iv. They are good conductors of heat and electricity.

d. The process of pouring out the upper layer of clear liquid without disturbing the sediment is called ___________.

i. sedimentation ii. evaporation
iii. decantation iv. distillation

e. Which of the following methods is used to separate scrap iron from a garbage heap?

i. Sieving
ii. Magnetic separation
iii. Sublimation
iv. Filtration

f. Sublimation can be used to separate a mixture of ___________.

i. sand and ammonium chloride
ii. sand and sugar
iii. iron fillings and salt
iv. stones and rice

2 Fill in the blanks.

a. A ___________ (compound/ mixture) is formed when two or more elements combine together chemically.

b. ___________ (Malleability/ Ductility) is the ability of metals to be beaten into thin sheets.

c. ___________ (Sublimation/ Evaporation) is a process of solids directly converting into gases.

d. Filtration is used when the substances to be separated are ___________ (soluble/insoluble) in a liquid.

e. A dissolved solid can be separated from its solution using the ___________ (evaporation/ sedimentation) method.

3 Write T for True and F for False.

a. The property of a compound is different from the properties of its constituent elements.

b. Metalloids have the properties of both metals and non-metals.

c. Sieving allows fine flour particles to remain in the sieve while the bigger impurities pass through the sieve.

d. Sedimentation is followed by decantation in the separation of solid–liquid mixtures.

e. The process of evaporation is used to obtain common salt from sea water.

4 Define the following terms.

a. Element b. Mixture
c. Metalloid d. Sieving
e. Filtration f. Sedimentation

5 Choose the odd one out. Give reasons for the choice.

a. Iodine, camphor, sugar, ammonium chloride

b. O, C, Au, Mg
c. Sugar solution, coffee, tea, coconut oil

6 Differentiate between the following.

a. Element and compound
b. Ductility and sonority
c. Sedimentation and decantation
d. Evaporation and filtration

7 Answer the following questions in brief.

a. Write any two characteristics of an element.
b. What is a chemical symbol? Write the chemical symbols of the following elements: nitrogen, calcium, boron, gold and argon.
c. How is sieving method used at construction sites?
d. Mention the appropriate methods for the separation of the following mixtures:
   i. A mixture in which the components have different sizes
   ii. A mixture that has components with different magnetic properties
e. What is the principle behind magnetic separation method?

8 Answer the following questions in detail.

a. Distinguish between compounds and mixtures.
b. Define mixture. What are the characteristics of mixtures?
c. Explain the method used to separate a mixture of sand and sugar.
d. List any five properties of metals and non-metals.
e. List the features of the modern method of representation of elements.
f. Explain the method of sublimation with an example.

9 Think and answer.

You are given a mixture of sugar, iron fillings and wheat. How will you separate all the three components in this mixture? Name the method(s) that can be used.

10 Project

1. Make a model of some compounds using plastic balls and sticks or molecular model kit to learn about the arrangement of atoms in them.
2. Visit a mineral water plant and find how water is purified before it is packed in bottles. Write a report on the whole process.

11 In the Library

Ask your teacher to show the periodic table of elements. Observe how each element is represented by a unique symbol. Learn the symbols of a few common elements.

Worksheet

❶ Subject Integration

a. Which of the following sources of water is used to obtain common salt and why?

River

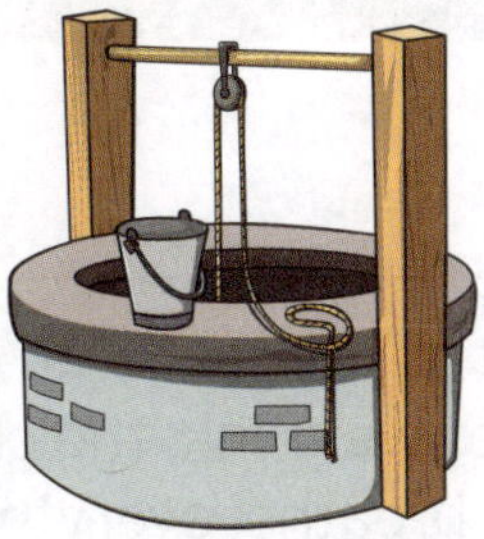

Well

Dam

Sea

____

b. Mention the separation technique and the principle used to obtain common salt from that source of water.

____

____

____

❷ Life Skills

Form small groups. Name the methods you would use to separate the components from the following mixtures.

- Group A - Mixture 1: Salt, sugar and cornstarch

  ____

- Group B - Mixture 2: Pebbles ,gravel, sawdust and sand

  ____

- Group C - Mixture 3: Sand, salt and pepper powder

  ____

- Group D - Mixture 4: Plastic beads, confetti balls and ball bearings

  ____

Matter

3

What I shall learn

- Properties of matter
- Composition of matter
- States of matter
- Effect of heat on matter

Introduction

All the things around us are made up of matter. Right from the food we eat, the water we drink, the chair we sit on, the books we read to the air we breathe, everything is made of matter. We, human beings, are also made up of matter. All the things mentioned above have mass and occupy a certain space. Therefore, **matter** can be defined as anything that has mass and occupies space.

Let us learn about the properties of matter and different states of matter in detail in this chapter.

Properties of Matter

Matter has the following properties.

- **Matter has mass**: When we carry an empty basket, it feels very light. When we fill the basket with books, toys and clothes, we find the basket quite heavy. This is because matter has mass. Let us do an activity to understand this concept.

Activity 1

Aim: To study that matter has mass

Materials required: Two paper bags, some marbles and a weighing balance

Procedure:

1. Weigh the two empty paper bags using a weighing balance.
2. Now add some marbles to one of the paper bags.

Observation: The paper bag that is filled with marbles becomes heavier when compared to the empty one.

Conclusion: Matter has mass.

- **Matter occupies space**: Take a deflated balloon and blow air into it. Air fills up the balloon. Now, try to fill air in an already blown-up balloon. Can we fill the same amount of air in this balloon also? No, because some air is already occupying space inside the balloon. In other words, matter occupies space. Similarly, our books occupy space in our bag. Our lunch occupies space in our lunch box. Let us do an activity to know about this concept.

▲ Air fills up the balloon

Activity 2

Aim: To study that matter occupies space

Materials required: Beaker, stone and water

Procedure:

1. Fill the beaker with water up to the brim.
2. Now, gently drop the stone into the beaker. The stone should be dropped from a reasonable height such that the beaker does not break.

Before After

Observation: The water spills out of the beaker.

Conclusion: Water occupies the space in the beaker. When the stone is dropped, the water spills out of the beaker to make room for the stone. Thus, we can conclude that matter occupies space.

We know that air has mass and anything that has mass exerts pressure. In other words, we can say that air exerts pressure. Let us understand this with the help of the following activity.

Activity 3

Aim: To take out an egg from a glass bottle without destroying it.

Materials required: A boiled egg, a glass bottle with an opening slightly narrower than the size of the egg

Procedure:

1. Place the empty glass bottle on a table.
2. Peel the boiled egg and place it on the mouth of the glass bottle.
3. Now carefully tilt the bottle and blow air into the mouth of the bottle.
4. Make sure to stand out of the way as the egg will pop right out of the bottle.

Observation and Conclusion: This activity is an example to show the behaviour of 'air pressure'. When we tilt the bottle and blow air into it, the air pressure inside the glass bottle increases which pushes the egg back out of its opening.

Composition of Matter

When people build walls and other structures using bricks, they place the bricks one over the other and add cement to bind the bricks. We can say that bricks are the building blocks of walls, houses and other buildings. A brick helps to make buildings, but what is a brick made of? To find out, break a brick into pieces. When we break it completely, we get a fine powder. Is a small grain of that powder, the smallest unit of a brick? No, the brick is made up of particles that are smaller than even a grain of powder.

The smallest particle that makes up a substance or matter is called an **atom**.

- An atom is the basic unit of an **element**, which represents a substance. Examples of elements are hydrogen, oxygen, gold and silver. Atoms retain the properties of their respective elements.
- When two or more atoms combine, they form a **molecule**. Molecules are made up of atoms of either the same kind or different kinds. Examples of molecules include hydrogen molecule and water molecule (containing hydrogen and oxygen atoms).
- Molecules formed from atoms of different kinds are called **compounds**. Water is a compound.

Intermolecular Distance and Intermolecular Force

Molecules are arranged in a particular manner in each substance. In some substances, molecules are arranged very closely with very less space between them and in some other substances, molecules are arranged far apart. The distance between the molecules of a substance is called **intermolecular distance**.

The molecules in a substance are held together by a force called **intermolecular force**. The stronger the intermolecular force, the closer are the molecules and the shorter is the intermolecular distance.

(a) Ice (solid)

(b) Water (liquid)

(c) Steam (gas)

▲ Three states of water

States of Matter

When we observe our surroundings, we find that matter exists in different forms. Collect and observe a few objects from your surroundings-wood, stone, ice cubes, metal spoon, water, milk, oil and an air-filled balloon. Some of these objects are solids, some are liquids while some are gases. Matter exists in three different states—solids, liquids and gases. But, what determines whether a substance exists in a solid, liquid or gaseous state? The existence of a substance in a particular state is determined by the properties of matter, which include the intermolecular force of attraction between the molecules. Some of these properties can be altered by a change in pressure or temperature.

Let us consider the example of water. Water exists in liquid state at room temperature. When we boil water at 100°C, it converts into steam, that is, its gaseous state. When liquid water is cooled to 0°C, it converts into ice, that is, its solid state. Let us learn more about each state of matter.

Solids

Observe the image of the chair given alongside. Does it have a definite shape? Yes, it has a definite shape. Even if we move it from one place to another, its shape remains the same. Also, it has a definite volume that never changes. A substance with a definite shape and volume is called a **solid**.

▲ A solid substance has a definite shape and volume

Solids are mostly hard and rigid. Due to this reason, it is not easy to compress solids. Solids have a fixed boundary, shape and volume. We can change the shape of some solids by applying force, but their volume will remain the same. For example, the shape of solids like a sponge changes when we compress them.

Arrangement of Molecules in Solids

In solids, the molecules are closely packed. This is because the intermolecular force between the molecules of solids is strong. Therefore, the molecules are not free to move around. This is the reason behind the fixed shape of solids.

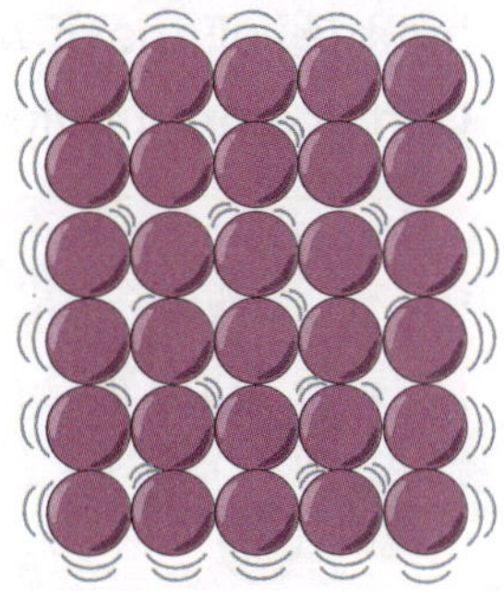

▲ Arrangement of molecules in solids

Properties of Solids

- The molecules in a solid are tightly packed.
- Solids have a definite shape and volume.
- Solids are hard and rigid.
- Solids are not easily compressible.
- Solids do not diffuse.

Liquids

We have learned that solids have a definite shape and size. What about liquids? What is the shape of a liquid? Take a conical flask and a beaker. Pour some water into the beaker first. Note the shape of the water. We can see that it takes the shape of the beaker. Now, pour the same amount of water into the conical flask. The water takes the shape of the conical flask. This means that water or any other liquid, in general, does not have a definite shape. It takes the shape of the container it is kept in. The amount of water in both the containers is the same. This means that water has a fixed or definite volume though its shape varies. A substance that has a definite volume but not a definite shape is called a **liquid**.

The shape of a liquid changes from container to container. This indicates that a liquid is not hard and rigid like a solid. A liquid is compressible to some extent, since the intermolecular distance in liquids is more than that in solids. Liquids have the ability to flow which makes them diffuse from

Science in Context

In a liquid and a gas, the molecules are loosely packed, so they have some regions with more molecules and other regions with fewer molecules. The movement of molecules from a region of higher concentration to a region of lower concentration is called **diffusion**. The movement of molecules continues until there is equal distribution in the medium. Diffusion allows molecules to spread out and mix with other molecules.

Activity 4

Aim: To understand that liquids have a definite volume but not a definite shape

Materials required: Glass bowl, glass tumbler, glass jug and water

Procedure:

1. Fill 50 mℓ water into the glass tumbler.
2. Observe the shape of the water.
3. Transfer the water into the bowl and observe the shape of the water.
4. Similarly, transfer the water into the jug and then observe the shape of the water.

A liquid takes the shape of the container it is stored in

Observation: The shape of water changes according to the shape of the vessel it is poured into, but the volume of water remains the same.

Conclusion: Liquids have a definite volume but not a definite shape.

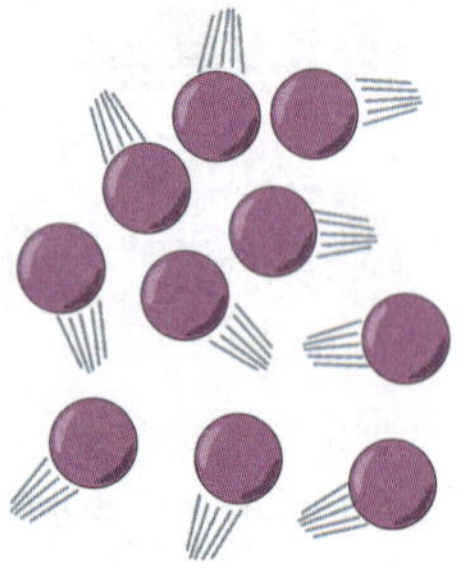

▲ Arrangement of molecules in liquids

Everyday Science

In an LPG cylinder, the gas inside the cylinder is in the liquid form under high pressure. When we turn on the knob of the cylinder, pressure is released from the liquid, which converts the liquid into the gaseous form.

▲ A gas takes the shape and volume of the tyre

one region to another. For example, if we put a drop of ink into a glass of water, it spreads uniformly and the water turns blue.

Arrangement of Molecules in Liquids

Liquids have a weaker intermolecular force between their molecules than solids. So, their intermolecular distance is more than that in solids. In other words, the molecules in liquids are less closely packed than in solids. Therefore, liquids are not rigid and hard like solids. The molecules in a liquid are loosely bound and can move around easily. This is the reason why liquids can flow.

Properties of Liquids

- In liquids, the molecules are loosely packed.
- Liquids do not have a definite shape but have a definite volume.
- Liquids are compressible unlike solids.
- Liquids diffuse slowly.
- Liquids flow from a higher level to a lower level.

Can you cut a solid, for example, an apple, using a knife? Yes, you can. Can you cut a liquid such as milk? No, because it has no definite shape and it flows.

Gases

When we fill a cycle tyre or a balloon with air, the gas (air) takes the shape and volume of the tyre and the balloon, respectively. This means that gases do not have a fixed shape.

Take a balloon and fill it with air. Then, prick the balloon to burst it. What happens to the air in it? We feel the air move out in all directions. This means that gases can move freely in all directions. Therefore, they can diffuse easily from one region to another. Gases are also highly compressible since their intermolecular distance is larger than that in solids and liquids. Thus, a **gas** is a substance that has neither a definite shape nor a definite volume.

Activity 5

Aim: To show that air does not have a definite shape

Materials required: Balloons of different shapes

Procedure:

1. Fill air in all the different-shaped balloons.
2. Then, deflate all the balloons.

Observation: Air takes the shape of the balloons it is blown into. It escapes when the balloons are deflated.

Conclusion: Air has no definite shape.

Balloons of different shapes

Science in Context

Both liquids and gases are called **fluids** as they are the states of matter that can flow.

Arrangement of Molecules in Gases

The intermolecular force between the molecules of gases is very weak. As a result, the gas molecules do not have contact with each other and can move around freely in any direction. Thus, the molecules in a gas are more loosely packed than in solids and liquids.

Properties of Gases

- The molecules of gases are very loosely packed.
- Gases neither have a definite shape nor a definite volume.
- Gases diffuse rapidly.
- Gases can be compressed to a high extent.

We can conclude that volume and shape of substances are the basic properties for their classification as solids, liquids or gases.

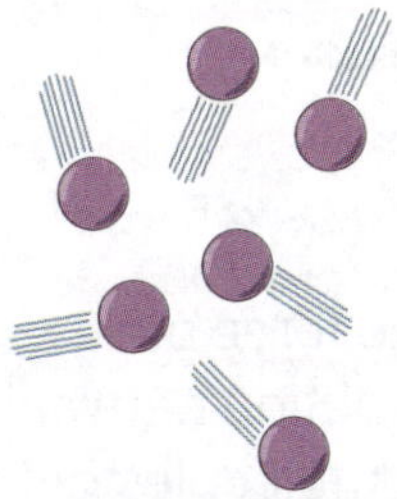

▲ Arrangement of molecules in gases

Activity 6

Aim: To demonstrate diffusion in solids, liquids and gases

Materials required: Mango juice, two glass beakers with water, stone and air freshener

Procedure:

1. Keep the beakers on a table. Drop the stone in the first beaker. Observe what happens to the stone.
2. Add two spoons of mango juice in the second beaker. Note the time in which the juice completely mixes with water.
3. Spray the air freshener in one corner of the room. Note the time taken for the smell to reach your friend at the opposite corner of the room.

Observation: The stone in the water remains as it is. The mango juice mixes with water in a minute or so. Your friend gets the smell of the air freshener in a few seconds.

Conclusion: Solids cannot diffuse. Liquids can diffuse. Gases diffuse the quickest.

Table 3.1 summarizes the differences in the properties of solids, liquids and gases.

Table 3.1 Differences in the properties of solids, liquids and gases

Property	Solids	Liquids	Gases
Arrangement of molecules	Tightly packed 	Loosely packed 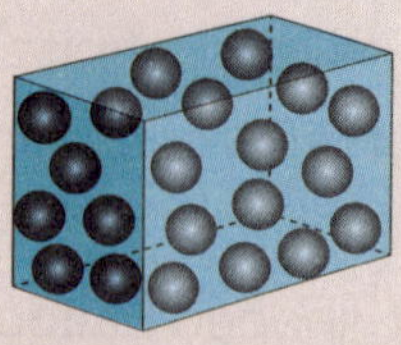	Very loosely packed 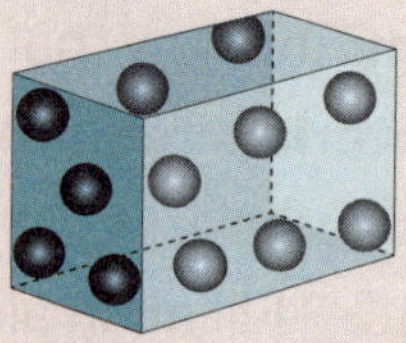
Intermolecular distance	Very small	More than in solids	More than in liquids and solids
Intermolecular force	Very strong	Weak	Very weak
Shape	Definite shape	No definite shape. It takes the shape of the container.	No definite shape. It takes the shape of the container.
Volume	Definite volume	Definite volume	No definite volume. It fills the volume of the container.
Ability to flow	Cannot flow	Flows from a higher level to a lower level	Flows in all directions
Diffusion	Does not occur	Can occur easily and slowly	Can occur very easily and quickly
Cohesive forces (The force of attraction between the molecules of the same substance is known as cohesive force.)	Very strong cohesive force Hence, the molecules in solids are arranged in fixed positions. Thus, solids have definite shape and volume.	Less cohesive force Hence, the molecules in liquids are arranged very close to one another. Due to the presence of the cohesive forces, liquids have definite volume. They do not have fixed shape and take the shape of the container they are poured into because the molecules in liquids undergo random motion	Negligible cohesive force Hence, the molecules in gases move in all possible directions. Thus, gases neither have fixed shape nor fixed volume.
Compressibility	Cannot be compressed Very less free space between the molecules of solids	Can be compressed to a small extent More free space between the molecules of liquids as compared to solids	Highly compressible Lot of free space between the molecules of gases

(Table 3.1 continued)

Property	Solids	Liquids	Gases
Brownian movement (The random motion that the molecules experience is known as Brownian movement, first observed by the scientist Robert Brown.)	Negligible molecular motion	Visible Brownian molecular motion	Free and random Brownian molecular motion

Activity 7

Aim: To understand the intermolecular space between the molecules/particles of solids and that smaller particles occupy spaces between bigger particles

Materials required: Two plastic beakers, sugar, pebbles (any shape), sand and glass balls (spherical in shape)

Procedure:

1. Take two clean plastic beakers or containers.
2. Add pebbles in one beaker and glass balls in the other beaker.
3. Now add sugar to the beaker containing pebbles and sand to the beaker containing glass balls.

Observation and Conclusion: We will observe that the smaller particles (i.e. sugar and sand) occupy spaces between the larger particles (i.e. pebbles and glass balls).

Also, more amount of sand is required to fill the beaker with glass balls than the amount of sugar required to fill the beaker with pebbles. As sand particles are small in size as compared to the sugar particles, they can fill up every available intermolecular space.

Revision Zone

Fill in the blanks.

1. An atom is the basic unit of a/an ____________ (element/compound).
2. The molecules of water are more ____________ (loosely/tightly) packed than the molecules of oxygen.
3. The ____________ (weaker/stronger) the intermolecular force, the shorter is the intermolecular distance.
4. Liquids have a weaker intermolecular force between their molecules than ____________ (solids/gases).

Effect of Heat on Matter

Expansion and Contraction

Substances can increase in size on heating. During heating, the particles (molecules) of the substances move apart (expand) and become loosely arranged. This kind of change is known as **expansion**.

Substances can decrease in size on cooling. During cooling, the particles (molecules) of substances move closer (contract) and become tightly packed. This kind of change is known as **contraction**.

The extent to which substances expand or contract differs for solids, liquids and gases. This is because of the difference in the way particles are arranged in each state. Table 3.2 gives a comparison between the three states.

Table 3.2 Expansion and contraction in solids, liquids and gases

Solids	Liquids	Gases
Expansion		
Least Example: Iron tools (e.g. trowel) are heated before they are fitted with wooden handles. Due to heating, the iron tools expand and the ring present at the centre of such tools increase in diameter. Thus, the wooden handles can be easily fixed into the ring.	Less Example: When milk boils, it spills out of the container if the burner is not turned off. This is due to expansion.	Most Example: Inflated balloons burst when kept in bright sunlight for a long time. This is because air absorbs heat from sun and expands. The expansion of air inside the balloon causes it to burst.
Contraction		
Least Example: As the iron tools cool, the ring contracts to its original diameter and fits firmly onto the wooden handle.	Less Example: When the burner is turned off, the heat supply is cut and the expansion stops. The milk begins to cool down. Due to cooling, the milk contracts and comes back to its previous level.	Most Example: If the inflated balloon is placed in a bowl containing cold water, the gases present inside the balloon will contract and the balloon will shrink in size.

Some applications of expansion and contraction in daily life are as follows:

1. Blacksmiths make iron tools by heating iron as it becomes soft on heating and can be beaten into desirable shapes.

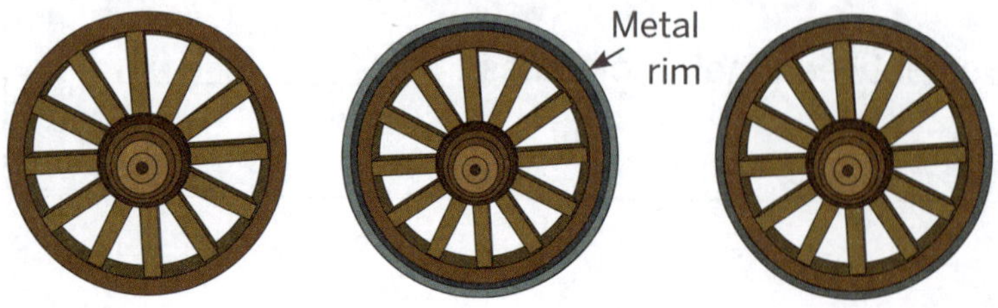

▲ Cartwheel

2. Metal rims on the wheels of a wooden cart can be fitted using the principle of contraction and expansion. On heating, the metal rim expands and easily slips onto the wheel. On cooling, the metal rim contracts and tightly fits onto the cartwheel.

▲ Gap between the rails

3. Railway tracks are laid with gaps in between them. If the railway tracks are fixed without any gaps, then during summer, due to expansion, they will expand and bend, and may cause accidents. Hence, gaps are left in order to allow expansion during hot weather.
4. Tightly jammed metal lids of food jars can be opened easily by pouring hot water over the lid or by dipping only the lid portion of the jar into hot water. As a result, the metal lid expands and opens easily.

▲ Food jar

Changes in States of Matter

It is possible to change the state of a substance. Let us understand this with the help of the following activity.

Activity 8

Aim: To study the change of state from a solid to liquid and from a liquid to gas

Materials required: Ice cubes, beaker, Bunsen burner and tripod stand

Procedure:

1. Place a few ice cubes in the beaker.
2. Keep the beaker over the tripod stand and heat it for a few minutes using the Bunsen burner. What do you observe?
3. Heat the beaker till the water boils off completely. What do you observe?

Observation: The ice cubes melt and convert into water upon heating in the first stage. Water converts into steam upon further heating in the second stage.

Conclusion: A solid converts into liquid upon heating and a liquid converts into gas upon further heating.

Melting The state of a substance depends on the arrangement of its molecules, that is, whether the molecules are closely packed or loosely packed. When certain solids are heated, the molecules in the solid vibrate and move away from each other. The intermolecular distance, thus, increases and when the intermolecular distance increases considerably, the solid matter is converted into its liquid state. This process in which solids get converted into liquids upon heating is called **melting**. Melting of butter and melting of ice are a few examples.

Vaporization or Boiling When liquids are heated, the molecules of liquids move further apart. At a certain point, the molecules move very far from each other and vibrate such that the liquid gets converted into its gaseous state. This process in which liquids get converted into gases upon heating is called **vaporization** or **boiling**.

Condensation When a gas is cooled, its vibrating molecules slow down as they lose the heat energy they had acquired during the heating process. As a result, the molecules move closer to each other and eventually the gas converts into liquid. This process in which gases get converted into liquids upon cooling is called **condensation**.

▲ Condensation

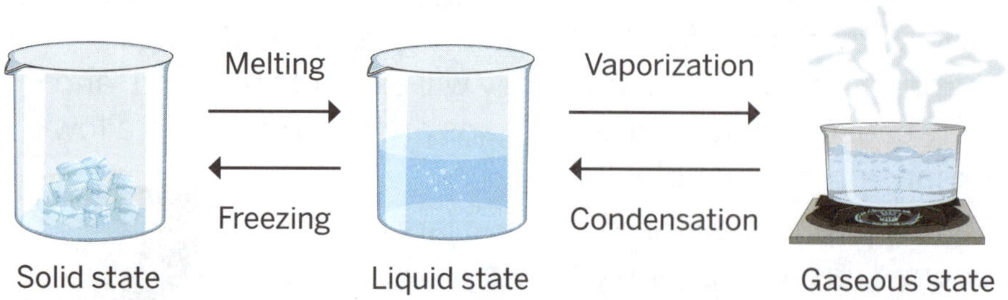

▲ Changes in the states of matter

Do You Know?

The volume of water expands by about 9 per cent when it freezes into ice.

Freezing When liquids are cooled, the vibration of their molecules slows down further. During this cooling process, the intermolecular distances reduce as the molecules settle. The molecules come closer together, thereby converting the liquid into solid. This process in which liquids get converted into solids upon cooling is called **freezing**. The figure given above summarizes the changes in the states of matter.

Sublimation Some solids get converted into gases upon heating without undergoing the liquid state. This process in which solids convert directly into gases without passing through the liquid state is called **sublimation**. Naphthalene and camphor are examples of solids that undergo sublimation.

Any substance on melting, boiling, condensation, freezing or sublimation undergoes physical changes. Changes in which no new substances are formed are known as **physical changes**. Such changes might alter the physical properties (like shape, size, colour, state or density) of the original substance. Chemical properties of the substance remain the same.
The change of state of matter is a physical change. It is a reversible and temporary change.

Chemical Changes

Changes in which new substances are formed are known as **chemical changes**. Such changes alter both physical and chemical properties of the original substances. For example, burning of paper, rotting of fruits and vegetables, baking of a cake, rusting of iron, process of digestion, photosynthesis and fermentation.

Characteristics of Chemical Changes

- New products are formed.
- The chemical composition and properties of the original substances change.
- All chemical changes are usually irreversible and permanent in nature.
- During a chemical change, energy is produced in the form of heat or light.

▲ Burning of wood

Examples of Chemical Changes

Burning of any substance When a log of a piece of wood or paper is burned, it combines with the oxygen in the air to form products like smoke, ashes, carbon dioxide and water vapour. Also, heat and light are released during this change. The properties of the new products formed are different from those of the original substances. We cannot get back wood or paper from the ashes. So, it is a permanent and an irreversible change.

Hence, burning of any substance is a chemical change.

Cooking of food While cooking food, heat energy is needed which results in the formation of new substances. Properties of the new substances are different from those of the original raw ingredients used for cooking and we cannot get back the raw ingredients. Hence, it is a chemical change.

▲ Cooked food

Revision Zone

Write T for True and F for False.

1. In a gas, diffusion takes place very slowly.
2. In a solid, the molecules are closely packed.
3. Liquids are compressible unlike the solids.
4. The process of gases converting into liquids upon cooling is called condensation.
5. Sublimation is the process in which a solid, on being heated, converts into its liquid state.

Keywords

Matter: Anything that has mass and occupies space

Physical change: Changes in which no new substances are formed

Chemical change: A change in which new substances are formed, and physical and chemical properties of the original substance are altered

Expansion: The increase in the size of a substance on heating

Contraction: The decrease in the size of a substance on cooling

In a Nutshell

- Anything that occupies space and has mass is called matter.
- Matter exists in three different states—solids, liquids and gases.
- Solids have a definite shape and volume. The molecules of a solid are closely packed.
- Liquids do not have a definite shape but have a definite volume. The molecules of a liquid are loosely packed.
- Gases neither have a definite shape nor a definite volume. The molecules of a gas are very loosely packed.
- The states of matter can be converted from one form to another through various processes like melting, freezing, vaporization, condensation and sublimation.
- Heating causes substances to expand and cooling causes them to contract.
- Chemical changes alter the physical as well as the chemical properties of the original substance.

Exercise

1 Choose the correct answer for each of the following.

a. Which of the following has a definite volume but not a definite shape?

i. Chair ii. Apple

iii. Oil iv. Soap bar

b. Gases occupy all the available space because their molecules are

i. strong ii. weak

iii. very loosely packed

iv. tightly packed

c. The process in which a gas converts into liquid upon cooling is called

i. vaporization ii. condensation

iii. melting iv. freezing

d. Fermentation is an example of

i. physical change

ii. chemical change

iii. change in pressure

iv. None of these

e. Heating makes the particles of a substance become

i. tightly packed

ii. stable

iii. loosely arranged

iv. None of these

f. The jammed metal cap of a glass bottle can be easily opened by

i. heating the cap

ii. cooling the cap

iii. heating the glass bottle

iv. cooling the glass bottle

2 Fill in the blanks.

a. Two or more atoms combine to form a _________ (compound/molecule).

b. The process of conversion of liquids into solids upon cooling is called _________ (sublimation/freezing).

c. If the chemical property of a substance changes, it is called a _________ change (chemical/physical).

d. The molecules of a substance move apart and become loosely arranged during _______ (contraction/expansion).

e. Substances decrease in size on _________ (heating/cooling) and contract.

3 Write T for True and F for False.

a. Gases can be compressed and stored in cylinders.

b. The process of conversion of solids into liquids upon heating is called vaporization.

c. Substances increase in size on heating.

d. Rusting of iron is an example of chemical change.

e. Sublimation is an example of physical change.

f. Iron becomes soft on cooling.

4 Complete the following.

a. Solid $\xrightarrow{\text{melting}}$ _______

b. Solid $\xrightarrow{?}$ Gas

c. _______ $\xrightarrow{\text{vaporization}}$ Gas

d. Liquid $\xrightarrow{?}$ Solid

e. Gas $\xrightarrow{\text{condensation}}$ _______

5. **Define the following terms.**
   a. Sublimation
   b. Vaporization
   c. Intermolecular force
   d. Condensation
   e. Diffusion
   f. Brownian movement

6. **Give an example for each of the following.**
   a. Condensation
   b. Sublimation
   c. Chemical change
   d. Expansion
   e. Contraction

7. **Differentiate between the following.**
   a. Melting and freezing
   b. Vaporization and condensation
   c. Elements and compounds
   d. Expansion and contraction
   e. An atom and a molecule

8. **Give reasons for the following.**
   a. Solids are hard and rigid.
   b. Liquids take the shape of the containers.
   c. Molecules in a gas can move around freely in any direction.
   d. Chemical changes are mostly permanent.
   e. In case of expansion, the size of a substance increases on heating

9. **Answer the following questions in brief.**
   a. What is matter and what are its properties?
   b. What is matter composed of?
   c. What is the difference between intermolecular distance and intermolecular force?
   d. What is cohesive force?
   e. Write any two properties of liquids.
   f. How do solid, liquid and gaseous substances show compressibility?
   g. What is physical change? Give an example.

10. **Answer the following questions in detail.**
    a. Explain the arrangement of molecules in solids, liquids and gases.
    b. Summarize the properties of solids, liquids and gases.
    c. Explain with the help of an activity how changes in the states of matter happen.
    d. List any three applications of contraction and expansion of substances in daily life.
    e. Define chemical change. Write the characteristics of a chemical change.

11. **Think and answer.**

A sponge is an example of solid though it is compressible. Is it an exception to the properties of solids or an illusion? Give reasons for your answer. (Hint: It has space to hold air.)

12. **Project**

Make a model with plastic balls and strings to show the arrangement of atoms in solids, liquids and gases.

13. **In the Library**

We have studied about three states of matter. But there are five states of matter—Solids, liquids, gases, plasma and Bose-Einstein condensates. Try to find how the molecules are arranged in the remaining two states of matter.

Worksheet

1 Subject Integration

a. Write the name of the process shown in the image given below. Also write the name of the states of matter that are involved in the given process.

____

____

b. Draw the arrangement of molecules in each state that get converted from one form to the other in the above process.

c. Mention the reason for the conversion of the change of state of matter.

____

____

2 Safeena has a metal ball and a ring. Before heating the metal ball, the ball could pass through the ring. Then, she heated the metal ball over a flame until it got very hot. She tried to pass the heated metal ball through the ring and found that the ball could not pass through the ring.

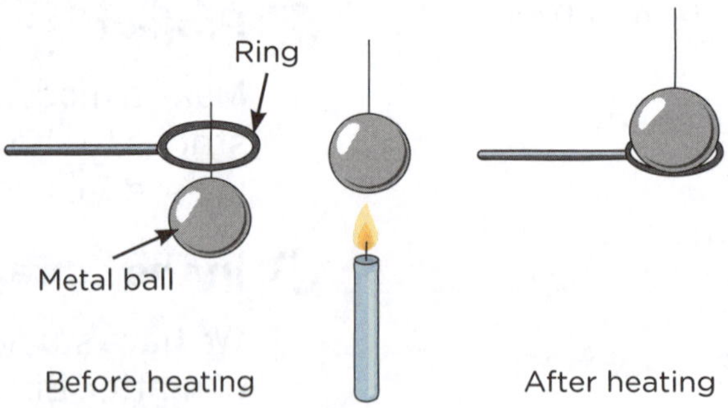

- What would Safeena conclude from this experiment?

____

- How can Safeena pass the metal ball through the ring once again?

____

Water

4

What I shall learn

- Uses of water
- Sources of water
- Water as the universal solvent
- Solubility
- Importance of water for sustenance of life on Earth
- Water pollution
- Conservation of water

▲ Water as a mode of transport for ships

Introduction

Water is one of the basic requirements of living things. Nearly 71 per cent of Earth's surface is covered with water. Of this, a major part (97 per cent) of the water on Earth is found in seas and oceans, but it is not suitable for drinking and other uses because it has a high salt content. The remaining 3 per cent of Earth's water is fresh water. A major part of the fresh water is frozen in glaciers and polar ice caps. Only less than 1 per cent of the total fresh water is available for human consumption. This fresh water is found below the ground or in lakes, rivers, streams, etc. That is why water is so precious!

Uses of Water

Water plays an important role in our day-to-day life. It has many important uses, some of which are discussed below.

- Water is used for various domestic purposes such as drinking, washing, bathing and cooking.
- Water drawn from rivers, bore wells and streams is used for agriculture (growing crops like rice, wheat, sugarcane and vegetables on a large scale).
- Water acts as a mode of transport for boats and ships.
- Water is used to generate electricity.
- Water serves as a raw material, ingredient and solvent in preparing various products in several industries.

Sources of Water

The main sources of water on Earth are rainwater, surface water and groundwater.

Rainwater Rainwater is the primary source of water. It is also considered the purest form of water. The water that evaporates from Earth's surface forms clouds. When these clouds get saturated, they pour down as rain. The evaporated water does not carry any salts or impurities. As a result, rainwater is pure, that is, without any impurities. But as it falls and passes through the atmosphere, it mixes with gases like sulphur dioxide and carbon dioxide, and impurities like smoke and dust particles which make it impure.

Surface Water Surface water refers to the water found on Earth's surface in the form of rivers, streams, lakes, ponds, seas and oceans. Some of the rainwater that falls on land flows into low-lying areas like ponds, rivers, lakes, etc. This water that flows off is called **runoff water**. The runoff water either flows into rivers or gets stored in lakes to form a freshwater source. In hilly regions, the runoff water flows from higher areas to form rivers that flow into valleys. Along with rainwater, melted water from snow caps and glaciers also contributes to the surface water as it flows into rivers and lakes. Rivers flow into seas or oceans. All these water sources form the surface water of Earth.

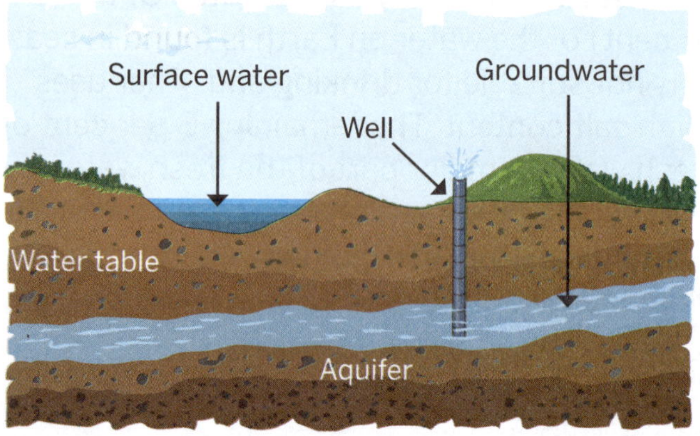

▲ Sources of water

Groundwater Rainwater and surface water seep through the soil below the ground and collect above gravel and non-porous rocks deep under the soil. The seepage of rainwater through the surface of the soil is called **infiltration**. The level below which soil is saturated with water is called the **water table**. An **aquifer** refers to the groundwater stored between the hard, rocky layers below the water table.

Groundwater can also be reached by digging wells. People depend on groundwater when there is shortage of surface water. Bore wells are constructed by boring a hole in the ground until the aquifer is reached. The pressure of groundwater is more at the aquifer and it comes out to the surface of Earth through natural openings or crevices of rocks in the form of natural springs.

Survey

Conduct a survey to know the different sources of water in your locality.

Water as the Universal Solvent

Water can dissolve a variety of substances in it and that is why it is considered a good solvent. Water is also known as the **universal solvent** because more substances can dissolve in it than in any other liquid.

You might have noticed the preparation of sugar syrup at home. When we add some sugar to water and mix it, the sugar disappears in the water. This is because the sugar dissolves in the water to form a sugar solution. Here the substance that dissolves, that is, sugar (smaller component) is the **solute** and the substance in which the solute dissolves, that is, water (larger component) is the **solvent**. The solute dissolves in the

Glucose solution Soft drink

▲ Solutions

solvent to form a **solution**. Thus, a solution is the uniform mixture of solute and solvent. Some common examples of solutions are as follows.

- In salt solution, salt (smaller component) is the solute and water (larger component) is the solvent.
- In glucose solution, glucose (smaller component) is the solute and water (larger component) is the solvent.
- In soda, carbon dioxide is the solute (smaller component) and water (larger component) is the solvent.

Let us perform an activity on preparation of copper sulphate solution.

Activity 1

Aim: To prepare the copper sulphate solution.

Materials required: Glass beaker, water, spatula, glass rod, copper sulphate crystals

Procedure:

1. Take 50 mℓ of water in a clean glass beaker.
2. Add two spatulas of copper sulphate crystals into the beaker containing water.
3. Using a glass rod stir the contents of the beaker until the copper sulphate crystals dissolve completely.

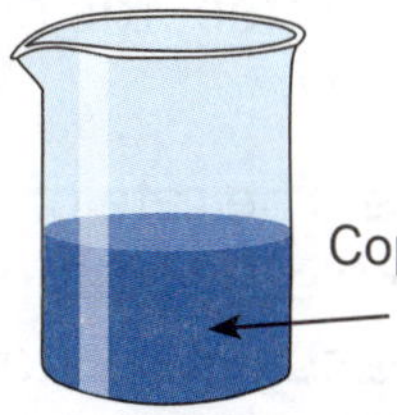

Observation: The copper sulphate crystals completely dissolve in water to form copper sulphate solution.

In Activity 1, water is the larger component and is referred to as the solvent. Copper sulphate crystals are the smaller component and are referred to as the solute.

All substances do not dissolve in water. For example, when salt is added to water and stirred, it dissolves completely in water, but when sand is added to water and stirred, it does not dissolve in water. Substances that dissolve completely in water are said to be **soluble** in water. Substances that do not dissolve in water are said to be **insoluble** in water.

Solubility

The property of a given substance to dissolve in a given liquid is called the **solubility** of that substance. The solubility of a solute is defined as the maximum amount of solute that dissolves in a given amount of solvent at a given temperature. The resulting solution is a saturated solution. Solubility is expressed in grams of solute per 100 g of solvent.

A solution in which no more solute can be dissolved in the solvent at a given temperature is called a **saturated solution**. Let us perform an activity to see how we can prepare a saturated solution.

> **Remember**
>
> A solution in which solute concentration is low and more solute can be dissolved in the solvent at a given temperature is called an **unsaturated** solution.

Activity 2

Aim: To prepare a saturated solution

Materials required: Beaker, water, common salt, glass rod and spatula

Procedure:

1. Take 50 mℓ of water in a clean glass beaker.
2. Add one spatula of salt and stir it well using a glass rod until the salt crystals dissolve completely.
3. Add one more spatula of salt and stir well.
4. Keep adding more salt, one spatula at a time, and stir each time. Observe what happens.

Observation: After adding a few spatulas of salt, despite stirring, some salt crystals are left undissolved at the bottom of the beaker.

Conclusion: No more common salt can be dissolved in the solution because the solution has become saturated. This is called a saturated solution.

Conditions Affecting the Solubility of a Solute

The factors that affect the solubility of a solute or the formation of a solution are as follows.

- **Temperature**: The rate of solubility of a solute in a solvent increases with an increase in temperature (i.e. by heating). For example, while preparing sugar solution, if the solution is heated, the sugar crystals dissolve quicker and also some more amount of sugar can be dissolved in the solution. In case of solids, the rate of solubility increases with increase in temperature, but for gases, the rate of solubility increases with decrease in temperature. Hence, soft drinks are stored at low temperatures to keep the gases dissolved.
- **Stirring**: It helps to dissolve the solute particles faster in a solvent.
- **Size of solute**: The smaller the size of the solute particles, the faster is the solubility of the solute in the solvent or the rate of formation of the solution. Consider the example of sugar cubes. If we add big sugar cubes in a beaker of water, they will take more time to dissolve in water than powdered sugar.
- **Chemical properties**: The solubility of a solute in a solvent also depends upon the chemical properties of both the solute and the solvent.

Activity 3

Aim: To study that an increase in temperature increases the rate of solubility

Materials required: Two beakers, spatula, common salt, Bunsen burner and stopwatch

Procedure:

1. Fill both the beakers with 50 mℓ water each.
2. Add one full spatula of common salt to each of the beakers.
3. Heat the solution in the second beaker on the Bunsen burner.
4. Note the time taken for the salt in both the beakers to dissolve with the help of a stopwatch.

Observation: The salt in the second beaker dissolves faster than that in the first beaker.

Conclusion: Increase in temperature increases the rate of solubility.

Activity 4

Aim: To study that stirring increases the rate of solubility

Materials required: Two glass beakers, spatula, common salt, glass rod and stopwatch

Procedure:

1. Fill both the beakers with equal amount of water, say 50 mℓ each.
2. Add one full spatula of common salt to each of the beakers.
3. Now, stir only the solution in the second beaker using a glass rod.
4. Note the time taken for the salt in both the beakers to dissolve with the help of a stopwatch.

Observation: The salt in the second beaker dissolves faster than that in the first beaker.

Conclusion: Stirring increases the rate of solubility.

Revision Zone

Fill in the blanks.

1. A river is an example of a ______________ (freshwater/groundwater) source.
2. The water that flows into rivers, streams, seas and oceans is called ______________ (runoff water/water table).
3. A ______________ (spring/lake) is a source of groundwater.
4. In glucose solution, glucose is the ______________ (solute/solvent).

Importance of Water for Sustenance of Life on Earth

▲ Water for drinking

Plants, animals and human beings need water for their survival. All living things require water to carry out various life processes in their body. Some of the uses of water are as follows:

- Water constitutes about 70 per cent of the human body. Animals and human beings need water for all their body functions like digestion, respiration, transport of nutrients to cells, excretion, etc. Water acts as a medium to dissolve nutrients and minerals present in the food we eat. This helps in the easy absorption of nutrients by our body. Water also dissolves waste materials produced inside the body which are then excreted as urine.
- Water helps in maintaining and regulating body temperature through sweating.
- Green plants require water during the process of photosynthesis to prepare their own food. Plants also require water to transport the prepared food from the leaves to the other plant parts. Water also plays a major role in the germination of seeds.
- All aquatic animals and plants require water to survive as they depend on nutrients and oxygen dissolved in water.

▲ Water for irrigation

Water Pollution

Water pollution refers to the contamination of water bodies due to which water becomes unsuitable for drinking, bathing, cooking and agricultural use.

Water is needed for drinking, bathing, washing and many other purposes. Due to an increasing population and rapid industrialization, the demand for water has gone up. But the availability of clean water for consumption is a problem due to the increased level of pollution in water bodies like rivers, lakes, ponds and groundwater. The impurities present in polluted water make it harmful for consumption by humans, animals and plants.

Causes of Water Pollution

Release of waste water into water bodies leads to water pollution. This adversely affects living things that live in and around water sources by causing diseases and bad odour. A few causes of water pollution are:

Domestic waste: Food wrappers, plastic covers, decayed food waste, metal cans, etc., are examples of domestic wastes. Disposal of these wastes into water bodies leads to contamination of water sources.

▲ Domestic waste

Industrial waste: The dumping of industrial waste into water bodies like lakes and rivers is one of the main causes of water pollution. This results in the release of toxic chemical compounds and gases into water bodies.

Toxic compounds like chromium, cadmium, lead, mercury and arsenic are released into water bodies along with toxic gases such as sulphur dioxide and nitrogen oxide.

▲ Discharge of sewage into water bodies

Sewage: Waste generated from household activities like washing, bathing, cleaning, etc., and human excreta is called sewage. When untreated sewage is released into rivers and lakes, harmful toxins and microorganisms present in it cause water contamination.

Agricultural waste: Fertilizers, insecticides and pesticides used in agricultural fields get washed off by rainwater into nearby water bodies and thus contaminate water. Such chemicals can also seep through the ground and pollute the groundwater.

Acid rain: Air pollutants like oxides of sulphur and nitrogen react with water vapour to form acids like sulphuric acid and nitric acid in the atmosphere. The sulphuric acid and nitric acid mix with rain to form acid rain. Acid rain changes the composition of water. It can harm plants and animals, and pollute soil and water bodies.

Thermal pollution: Nuclear and thermal power plants use water as a coolant in various processes. This produces hot

Do You Know?

On 17th January 2015, an oil spill occurred in the Yellowstone river at Montana, USA. Around 160 tonnes of oil spilled into the river and a cancer-causing agent called benzene was also released. Even after purification, the river water was found to contain impurities and toxins.

water that is let off into water bodies. The hot water changes the temperature of the water bodies. This type of pollution is known as thermal pollution.

Oil spills: The leakage of oil from shipping tankers or ships leads to the pollution of sea water.

Effects of Water Pollution

Polluted water causes infections and life-threatening diseases in living organisms. Some of the harmful effects of water pollution are the following:

- Discharge of domestic waste into water bodies leads to contamination of water. Thus, it adversely affects the living organisms that consume this polluted water. It also kills aquatic life.
- Industrial waste released into water bodies contains toxic compounds and gases which cause health complications in living organisms and harm aquatic plants and animals.
- Thermal pollution changes the temperature of water bodies, which affects aquatic plants and animals because the oxygen content in water decreases. The sudden variation in temperature kills many fish and other aquatic organisms. This is called **thermal shock**.
- Untreated sewage consists of many microorganisms like bacteria, viruses, fungi and parasites. These microorganisms can cause harmful diseases such as diarrhoea, dysentery, cholera and typhoid when water from such sources is used for human activities.
- When water from agricultural fields flow to rivers and lakes, the nutrients present in fertilizers cause the growth of algae in water bodies. Algae cover the entire surface of water bodies. This leads to depletion of oxygen in water, and also prevents sunlight from reaching aquatic plants and animals thus leading to their death. This is known as **eutrophication**.
- Oil spills form a layer of oil on the water surface in oceans and seas. This restricts sunlight from entering water bodies, which affects aquatic life.

▲ Eutrophication of lake

▲ Oil spill

Methods to Prevent Water Pollution

Prevention of water pollution includes conservation of water that is available for the ever increasing human population. A few methods that can be followed are given below:

- Government should impose strict laws against disposal of waste or sewage by industries, hospitals, markets, etc., which can help minimize water pollution. Fines should be levied on lawbreakers.
- The general population should be educated about the dangers of water pollution, and how to prevent it by organizing awareness programmes and workshops.

Greenathon

Rainwater harvesting is a method of collecting and storing rainwater. This water can be used for many domestic purposes like washing, irrigation, etc. It can also be used to replenish groundwater. Government policies should encourage the practice of rainwater harvesting by making it a mandatory requirement in houses and buildings in urban areas.

- Domestic sewage should be treated before being let off into the water bodies. Instead of synthetic detergents, biodegradable detergents should be used to reduce water pollution.
- Toxic chemicals and wastes released from industries should be treated before being disposed of into water bodies.
- Modern irrigation methods like drip irrigation and sprinkler irrigation should be used instead of flooding the fields with water. Flooding the fields with water leads to runoff water that carries fertilizers with it and pollutes the nearby water bodies.
- Use of biodegradable fertilizers and pesticides should be encouraged in order to avoid accumulation of harmful chemicals in the soil and water.

Conservation of Water

Only a small percentage of water on Earth is available for use. Therefore, water should be used judiciously and it should be conserved. We cannot create natural water resources.

The only way to meet the increasing demand is through judicious use and conservation of the available resources. **Conservation** is avoiding the wastage or loss of the important and precious resources necessary for future use.

- One of the best ways to conserve water is by minimal usage of water at home. Following are the ways by which wastage of water can be avoided at home.
  - Bathe using water in a bucket and avoid using the shower or bathtub. This will save water since using a shower or bathtub consumes a large amount of water.
  - Turn off the water tap when not in use, especially while brushing your teeth.
  - Take water in buckets and use a mug for watering the plants instead of using a hose to avoid excessive use of water.
  - Fix leaking taps and pipes. Leaking taps are one of the main causes of water wastage at home.

▲ Various methods of conservation of water at home

- A lot of rainwater goes into drains during the rainy season. This water can be conserved for future usage or to replenish the groundwater levels by the method of **rainwater harvesting**.

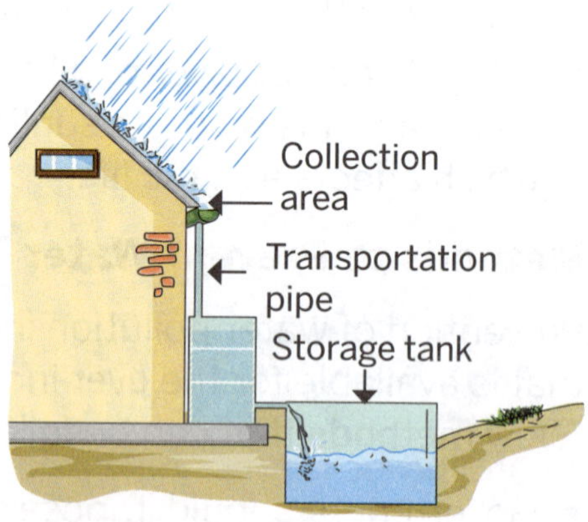

▲ Rainwater harvesting at home

Rainwater is collected from the rooftops through pipes and allowed to flow into a tank containing sand and gravel to filter the water. This water is then allowed to percolate through the soil. This recharges the water table that declines due to excessive usage of groundwater. Another method is collecting rainwater through pipes in a tank and using it for washing purposes at homes.

- Another simple but effective method to reduce the usage of water is by recycling the waste water from industries.

Do You Know?

In 2003, rainwater harvesting was made compulsory by law in Tamil Nadu. The government made it mandatory for all the buildings to have rainwater harvesting throughout the state. It was implemented not only in the new but also in the existing, old buildings.

This initiative by the Tamil Nadu government helped in improving the groundwater table as well as the quality of groundwater.

- Proper storage, management and distribution of water from sources such as rivers and lakes should be undertaken by constructing dams, reservoirs and pipelines.
- Drip irrigation in the agricultural lands can save a lot of water. In the drip irrigation method, crops and plants are given sufficient amount of water without any wastage.
- Planting trees and increasing the forest cover would lead to good rainfall and less pollution.

▲ Dam

▲ Drip irrigation

Keywords

Runoff water: Rainwater that falls on land and flows into rivers, streams and oceans

Water table: The level under the ground where the space between soil particles and rocks is filled with water

Infiltration: The seepage of rainwater through the surface of the soil

Aquifer: The groundwater stored between the hard rocky layers below the water table

Solubility: The ability of a substance to dissolve in a given liquid

Saturated solution: A solution in which no more solute can be dissolved in the solvent at a given temperature

Thermal pollution: The sudden variation in temperature of water in water bodies which adversely affects aquatic life

Eutrophication: A form of water pollution in which nutrient-rich fertilizers run-off along with water and cause excessive algal growth in water bodies

In a Nutshell

- All living organisms require water to carry out their life processes.
- Rainwater, surface water and groundwater are the three main sources of water.
- Water is is called the universal solvent.
- A solute dissolves in a solvent to form a solution.
- Polluted water has harmful effects on living organisms. It causes infections and life-threatening diseases.
- The main sources of water pollution are releasing untreated domestic waste, industrial waste, sewage and agricultural waste into water bodies, and oil spills.
- We must conserve water as it is precious.

Exercise

1 Choose the correct answer for each of the following.

a. Ocean water is an example of ________.

i. fresh water ii. groundwater
iii. surface water iv. potable water

b. The level below which soil is saturated with water is called ________.

i. water table ii. aquifer
iii. spring iv. well

c. Which of the following factors does not affect the solubility of a solute in a solvent?

i. Colour of the solute
ii. Size of the solute
iii. Temperature
iv. Chemical properties of both the solute and the solvent

d. Which of the following is not a cause of water pollution?

i. Acid rain ii. Oil spill
iii. Sewage iv. UV rays

e. Identify the method that helps to prevent water pollution.

i. Use of biodegradable fertilizers and pesticides
ii. Release of untreated industrial waste
iii. Wastage of water due to leaking taps at home
iv. Encourage the use of synthetic detergents

f. Which of the following is not a method of proper water management?

i. Construction of dams
ii. Construction of reservoirs
iii. Rainwater harvesting
iv. Construction of water parks

2 Fill in the blanks.

a. ________ (Rainwater/Runoff water) is the primary source of water.

b. The ability of a substance to dissolve in a given liquid is called ________ (solubility/sedimentation).

c. Acid rain contains oxides of ________ (sulphur/helium).

d. The sudden variation of temperature in water bodies that adversely affects aquatic life is called ________ (thermal shock/oil spill).

e. The smaller component present in a solution is referred to as ________ (solvent/solute).

3 Write T for True and F for False.

a. All the water found on Earth is suitable for drinking.

b. The seepage of rainwater through the surface of the soil is called infiltration.

c. The rate of solubility of gases increases with an increase in temperature.

d. A solution in which no more solute can be dissolved in a solvent is called a saturated solution.

e. Eutrophication indicates that the water source is pollution-free.

f. Water pollution can be reduced by treating the sewage before letting it off into water bodies.

4 Define the following terms.

a. Runoff water

b. Aquifer

c. Thermal pollution

d. Eutrophication

5 Differentiate between the following.

a. Surface water and runoff water

b. Solvent and solute
c. Soluble and insoluble substances
d. Saturated solution and unsaturated solution

6 Answer the following questions in brief.

a. Write any three uses of water in our everyday life.
b. What are the main sources of water on Earth? Give examples.
c. What is infiltration?
d. Why is water known as the universal solvent?
e. How does stirring affect the formation of a solution?
f. What is acid rain? What are its harmful effects?

7 Answer the following questions in detail.

a. Explain the importance of water to living things.
b. Define solubility and describe the factors that affect solubility.
c. What is water pollution? What are its different causes?
d. Mention the harmful effects of water pollution.
e. How can we prevent water pollution? Suggest different measures.
f. List any four ways to conserve water.

8 Think and answer.

a. Three-fourths of the Earth is covered with water, but only a very small percentage of water is available in usable form while all other water is salty. Why?
b. In a village, some of the wells ran dry. What could be the reason behind this?

9 Project

Conduct a water audit

Conduct a water audit at your home.

Prepare a table of the amount of water used (approximate) for different purpose at home; drinking, bathing, washing, toilets, cleaning floors, car washing, etc. per day. After the audit is complete, discuss with other students in class and identify ways to reduce water consumption at home.

10 In the Library

a. The tap water that we receive at home is obtained after many purification techniques. Collect information on the various steps involved in the process of water purification.
b. Read about rainwater harvesting. Find out how such arrangements can be installed and how it helps in water conservation.

Worksheet

1 Subject Integration

All living things need water for their survival. Human intervention in the natural resources has affected the life on Earth. Write an article for a student magazine describing how human intervention has led to shortage of water that is fit for domestic purposes, and its causes and effects. Also mention the remedies for the same.

2 Life Skills

It is important to have clean drinking water. Make sure that the water bodies in your surroundings are kept and maintained neatly. Do not throw waste in the water bodies and pollute them. Create awareness among others who pollute the water bodies. Save water! Save life!

Write any three measures that can be taken to raise awareness of conserving water bodies among the people in your locality.

Air and Atmosphere

5

What I shall learn

- Composition of air
- Importance of air
- Rusting
- Atmosphere

Introduction

Air is an important natural resource available on Earth. Air is present all around us as well as inside our body. Air has mass and occupies space. All livings things require air to survive.

We cannot see air but we can feel it. We can feel the presence of air when there is movement of things around us. The movement of a kite and the rustling of leaves prove that air is around us.

Composition of Air

In ancient days, air was believed to be an element or a pure substance. In the eighteenth century, scientists started to study the composition of air. Scientists like Antoine Lavoisier, Joseph Priestley and Henry Cavendish were the first to study the composition of air. Antoine Lavoisier discovered that oxygen plays a crucial role in combustion. Later, Joseph Priestley discovered oxygen and isolated it in its gaseous form. All such discoveries proved that air is a mixture of gases. The gases are present in the air in uniform composition. Hence, air is a homogeneous mixture of gases.

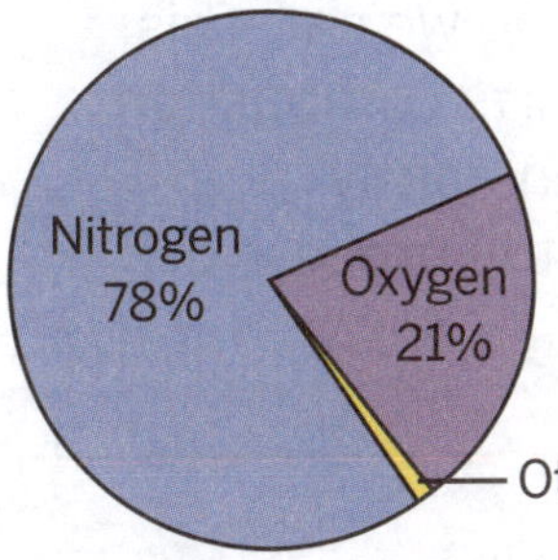

▲ Composition of air

Air mainly consists of gases, namely nitrogen (around 78 per cent), oxygen (around 21 per cent), carbon dioxide (around 0.03 per cent) and inert gases (around 0.9 per cent). Apart from these gases, small quantities of water vapour, dust and smoke are also present in air. The amount of these components varies in different regions from time to time. Figure above shows the composition of air. Table 5.1 gives the percentage by volume of the various components of air.

Table 5.1 Components of air and their percentage

Components of air	Percentage by volume
Nitrogen	78%
Oxygen	21%
Carbon dioxide	0.03%
Inert gases such as argon, helium, neon, krypton, etc.	0.9%
Water vapour	Varies
Others like dust, smoke, pollutants, etc.	Varies

Each component of air has its own properties and each retains its individual properties. The components of air do not react with each other. The composition of air varies from place to place and from season to season. For example, the amount

Do You Know?

Mountaineers carry oxygen cylinders with them. This is because the atmosphere extends only up to a few kilometres above the Earth's surface and the amount of oxygen goes on decreasing as we go up to higher altitudes.

Know the Scientist

Joseph Priestley (1733–1804) was an English chemist. He is credited for the isolation and discovery of oxygen in its gaseous state. He named it as 'dephlogisticated air'. He also synthesized nitrous oxide (laughing gas).

Science in Context

Carbon dioxide is used in fire extinguishers. We know that oxygen is required to burn a fuel. To extinguish fire, one has to cut off the supply of oxygen. Carbon dioxide forms a layer around the fuel and prevents the fuel from coming in contact with oxygen.

of water vapour in the air is more in coastal regions than in deserts. Hence, we cannot represent air with a chemical formula. Cities have a high amount of air pollutants due to increased dust and smoke released from vehicles, factories, etc. Let us now learn more about the different components of air.

Nitrogen

Nitrogen is the most abundant gas in the atmosphere. It is colourless and odourless. It is also called an inactive gas. Nitrogen does not support combustion. Nitrogen forms the basic building blocks of proteins in the bodies of all organisms. It is essential for plant growth and development. Some bacteria present in the soil convert atmospheric nitrogen into compounds which can be taken up and used by plants. Animals obtain nitrogen from plant and animal sources of food.

Oxygen

Oxygen is the second most abundant gas in the atmosphere. It is a chemically reactive gas. All living organisms such as fish, animals, insects, birds and human beings breathe in oxygen. Thus, oxygen is required by all living things to survive.

Oxygen is used to obtain energy from the food we eat. This process is called **respiration**. Oxygen supports combustion and is thus required to burn fuels. Plants constantly replenish oxygen in the atmosphere during the process of photosynthesis.

Activity 1

Aim: To show that oxygen is necessary for burning

Materials required: Two candles, jar or glass and matchstick

Procedure:

1. Place the two candles on a table and light them.
2. After a while, invert the jar or glass over one of the candles.

Observation: The candle which is exposed to air continues to burn, whereas the candle covered by the glass burns for a short while and then stops burning.

Conclusion: When the oxygen available inside the inverted glass is completely used up for burning, the candle stops burning. This proves that oxygen is necessary for burning.

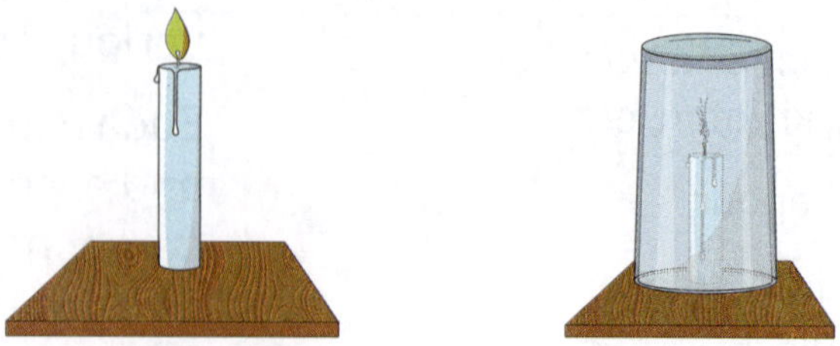

Carbon Dioxide

Air contains around 0.03 per cent of carbon dioxide. Carbon dioxide is also a chemically reactive gas. Though the percentage of carbon dioxide is less than 1 per cent, it is a vital component of the atmosphere. Carbon dioxide does not support combustion. Carbon dioxide is released by living things during respiration. It is also released during combustion of substances.

Carbon dioxide is used by plants to prepare food during photosynthesis. **Photosynthesis** is an important process as it involves consumption of carbon dioxide and release of oxygen. A slight increase in the percentage of carbon dioxide increases the overall temperature of Earth. This condition is known as **global warming**.

Inert Gases

Inert gases are a group of gases that are non-reactive and stable. These are also called **noble gases**. They are present in traces in air. These gases can be isolated from air. Argon, neon, helium, krypton, xenon and radon are common inert gases present in air. Argon, krypton, neon and xenon are mostly used for lighting purposes like in advertising sign boards, light bulbs and lamps. Helium is used in hot-air balloons. Radon is used in the treatment of cancer.

Water Vapour

The amount of water vapour present in the air in a particular place is known as **atmospheric humidity**. Evaporation from water bodies and transpiration from plants are the two sources of water vapour. Water vapour keeps the air cool and is also a part of the water cycle. It helps in the formation of clouds, which bring rain and act as an important source of water for all living things. As a result, water vapour is also responsible for climatic changes.

The amount of water vapour present in the air is not constant at all places. Coastal regions have high amounts of water vapour due to evaporation from the sea. Inland regions have high amounts of water vapour only during the rainy season.

Everyday Science

Air conditioners (ACs) work on the principle of changing the properties of air in the surroundings. That is, the temperature and humidity of air is changed. This makes the surroundings cooler.

Activity 2

Aim: To prove that water vapour is present in air

Materials required: A plastic bottle filled with water

Procedure:

1. Place the water bottle in a refrigerator.
2. Take out the bottle after 10–12 hours.
3. Observe the bottle after 5–10 minutes.

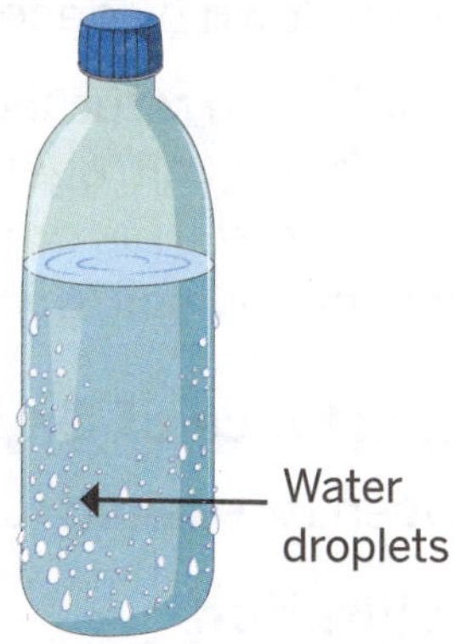

Observation: Water droplets appear on the outer surface of the bottle.

Conclusion: The water droplets are formed due to the water vapour present in the atmosphere. The water vapour condenses on the cool surface of the bottle.

Dust and Smoke

When we switch on a torch in a dark room and observe the beam of light, we see dust particles floating in the air. This means air also contains dust. Human activities have led to a huge increase in the amount of dust and smoke in the atmosphere. Dust and smoke are released during burning of fuels in vehicles and factories, construction of buildings, burning of garbage, using firewood for cooking, etc. Dust and smoke cause many respiratory diseases and allergies in human beings. These are present in higher amounts in cities than in villages.

Revision Zone

Write T for True and F for False.

1. The percentage of carbon dioxide present in the atmosphere is 21 per cent.
2. Oxygen does not support combustion.
3. Carbon dioxide is used by plants during photosynthesis.
4. Dust and smoke are released from factories and by burning of garbage.

Importance of Air

All living things need air to survive. Each component of air is is useful for living things. Air is necessary for many physical and chemical processes occurring around us. Let us discuss the importance of each gas in detail.

Importance of Nitrogen

Nitrogen is essential for all forms of life on Earth as it forms the building blocks of proteins. Nitrogen is required by plants for their growth, but plants cannot obtain nitrogen directly from the air. Nitrogen in the air is converted into a more usable form (nitrates and nitrites) through a series of chemical reactions whenever there is both lightning and rain. This way, nitrogen is introduced into the soil. Also, some bacteria present in the soil and in the roots of plants help to convert atmospheric nitrogen into usable forms. These usable forms of nitrogen are then absorbed by the roots of plants.

Animals get nitrogen for their needs by eating plants. When plants and animals die, their remains get mixed with the soil and are decomposed by bacteria present in the soil. This process helps in returning the nitrogen to the soil. Waste matter excreted by animals is also broken down by decomposers (bacteria and fungi) to return nitrogen to the soil.

The nitrogen returned to the soil (in the form of nitrites and nitrates) can also be converted into gaseous nitrogen by denitrifying bacteria present in the soil and released into the atmosphere. This complete process in which nitrogen is circulated in nature between the atmosphere, soil, microorganisms, plants and animals is known as the **nitrogen cycle**.

Importance of Oxygen

Oxygen is required for various processes. Let us look at each process in detail.

Respiration

All living things require oxygen to respire in order to stay alive. Respiration is a chemical process that takes place in all living cells of the body, all the time.

Living things inhale air that is rich in oxygen. The oxygen is used by the body to burn or break down food in order to produce energy. This energy is needed by the organism to carry out various life processes or activities. The process of burning or breakdown of food in the presence of oxygen to produce energy is known as **respiration**.

> **Remember**
>
> The air we breathe in is known as **inhaled air**. The air we breathe out is known as **exhaled air**.

The food we consume is digested and broken down into the simplest form called **glucose**. This glucose is carried to the cells by the blood. In the cells, the release of energy takes place with the help of oxygen. Glucose combines with oxygen to produce energy, releasing carbon dioxide and water vapour as by-products. The carbon dioxide thus produced is exhaled during breathing. So, the exhaled air contains more carbon dioxide than the air we breathe in.

Respiration can be represented by the following equation:

Glucose + Oxygen ⟶ Carbon dioxide + Water vapour + Energy
(from food)

Combustion or Burning of Fuels

Combustion is a chemical process in which a substance combines with oxygen (present in air) to produce new substances and release energy in the form of heat and light. Any substance that is burned in air to give out heat and light is called a **fuel**. Fuels burn in the presence of oxygen to produce carbon dioxide and water vapour as by-products and release energy in the form of heat and light.

Fuel + Oxygen $\xrightarrow{\text{heat}}$ Carbon dioxide + Water vapour + Energy

The energy produced during combustion or burning of fuels is used to cook food, to run automobiles, to produce energy in industries and for various other purposes.

Fuels are of different types based on their physical state, namely, solid fuels, liquid fuels and gaseous fuels. Some of the commonly used fuels are as follows.

Solid fuels These are fuels that exist in the solid state at room temperature.

- **Wood**: Dry wood is commonly used for cooking purposes. It is a cheap and easily available fuel. Burning of wood releases large amounts of carbon dioxide and water vapour.
- **Coal**: Coal is a fossil fuel. It is formed from the remains of dead plants over millions of years. Coal is mainly composed of carbon and it produces a large amount of heat energy on burning.

  Carbon + Oxygen ⟶ Carbon dioxide

  Coal is mostly used to produce electricity. Burning of coal releases carbon dioxide, compounds of nitrogen and sulphur, ash and smoke. These by-products lead to pollution of air.

▲ Burning of wood

Liquid fuels These are fuels that exist in the liquid state at room temperature.

- **Petroleum fuels**: Like coal, petroleum fuels (petrol, diesel, kerosene) are also fossil fuels. Petroleum has been formed from dead remains of sea organisms that got buried under sand and rocks over millions of years. Petrol and diesel are primarily used in automobiles as fuel. Kerosene is used in lamps and cooking stoves. Burning of these fuels also releases heat energy and a large amount of carbon dioxide, smoke and water vapour, which cause air pollution.

Gaseous fuels These are fuels that exist in the gaseous state at room temperature.

- **Liquefied petroleum gas (LPG)**: LPG is the most widely used fuel at home for cooking. It is usually stored in cylinders in the liquid state under pressure. The cylinders are connected to gas stoves. When the knob of the cylinder is turned on, the pressure is released and gas escapes through the pipe to reach the burner. LPG is considered a cleaner fuel because it produces fewer pollutants than other fuels and releases more heat energy.
- **Compressed natural gas (CNG)**: CNG is mainly used as a fuel in automobiles. It is compressed and stored in cylinders. CNG is cheaper and a cleaner fuel as it releases fewer pollutants into the air. Hence, nowadays, it is replacing petroleum fuels in automobiles.

Remember

Chlorophyll is a green-coloured pigment present in plants which helps to trap sunlight.

Both LPG and CNG produce carbon dioxide and water vapour on combustion.

Importance of Carbon Dioxide

Carbon dioxide is used for various processes. Let us look at them in detail.

Photosynthesis

Plants are the main source of food for all living things, including humans. Carbon dioxide is an essential gas for green plants. Green plants make use of carbon dioxide to prepare their own food through the process of photosynthesis. In the process of photosynthesis, green plants utilize carbon dioxide and water in the presence of sunlight and chlorophyll to produce food.

▲ Photosynthesis takes place in the presence of sunlight

In this process, food is obtained in the form of glucose which is stored by plants as starch. During photosynthesis, oxygen is given out as a by-product. This oxygen is used by both plants and animals for respiration. Aquatic plants make use of dissolved carbon dioxide to prepare their food and release oxygen. The reaction involved in photosynthesis is:

Challenge Yourself

You know that carbon dioxide can turn lime water milky. If you keep fresh lime water in a glass bowl in open air, will it turn milky?

$$\underset{\text{(from air)}}{\textbf{Carbon dioxide}} + \underset{\text{(from soil)}}{\textbf{Water}} \xrightarrow[\textbf{Sunlight}]{\textbf{Chlorophyll}} \underset{\textbf{(Glucose)}}{\textbf{Food}} + \textbf{Oxygen}$$

Balance of Carbon Dioxide and Oxygen in Nature

Photosynthesis and respiration are the two main processes that help in maintaining the balance of oxygen and carbon dioxide in nature. We know that oxygen is required for the survival of

Greenathon

Plant a sapling each year on your birthday. By doing so, you can grow trees, thus helping to make a green environment.

all living things. Imagine what would happen if all the oxygen is used up? Then there would be shortage of oxygen. But this does not happen because of plants and trees in nature. They are the oxygen suppliers. During photosynthesis, oxygen is produced and released into the atmosphere. This oxygen is used by both plants and animals for the process of respiration. During respiration, carbon dioxide is released into the atmosphere. Photosynthesis occurs only during the day due to requirement of sunlight, while respiration in plants occurs both day and night. Hence, this way oxygen–carbon dioxide balance is maintained in nature.

Even during combustion of fuels, oxygen is consumed and carbon dioxide is released in large amounts into the atmosphere.

Global Warming

It is a condition caused by the greenhouse effect in which the surface temperature of Earth increases due to the presence of greenhouse gases in the atmosphere. These greenhouse gases trap radiated heat energy from of the sun and warm up the Earth's surface even more. Greenhouse gases are released due to burning of fuels. Carbon dioxide is the main greenhouse gas.

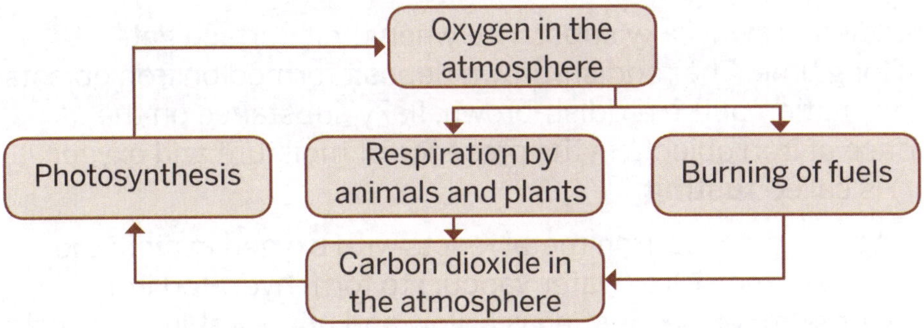

▲ Balance of oxygen and carbon dioxide in nature

Activity 3

Aim: To prove that air contains carbon dioxide

Materials: Glass beaker/tube, straw and some fresh lime water (calcium hydroxide)

Procedure:

1. Take some fresh lime water in the glass beaker/tube.
2. With the help of the straw, blow air into lime water.

Observation: The lime water turns milky.

Conclusion: Carbon dioxide turns lime water milky. Hence, we can conclude that air contains carbon dioxide.

Table 5.2 lists the processes in nature that maintain the balance of oxygen and carbon dioxide.

Table 5.2 List of processes that maintain the balance of oxygen and carbon dioxide

	Processes
Use oxygen	Respiration, rusting, burning of fuels, decomposition of organic matter
Release oxygen	Photosynthesis
Use carbon dioxide	Photosynthesis, absorption by water in water bodies like oceans
Release carbon dioxide	Respiration, combustion or burning of fuels, fermentation, volcanic eruptions, decomposition of organic matter

Harmful human activities disturb the balance in nature. Increasing population and industrialization require cutting down of trees (deforestation) and conversion of forest lands to set up factories and cities. Thus, green cover is lost which leads to alteration of oxygen levels in the atmosphere. Burning of fossil fuels releases carbon dioxide, carbon monoxide and other poisonous gases. Hence, all this results in increased levels of harmful gases in nature, leading to a condition called **global warming**.

As we know, oxygen is an important gas. To prevent an imbalance of oxygen–carbon dioxide in nature, the following measures can be taken.

- We should prevent the loss of green cover by planting more saplings. We must encourage afforestation and discourage deforestation.
- Encourage carpooling as this decreases the number of vehicles on the road and thus reduces the release of poisonous gases to some extent.
- Replace fossil fuels like petrol and diesel with cleaner fuels like CNG.

Rusting

Iron objects get covered with a reddish-brown, flaky substance when their surface gets exposed to air and moisture for a long time. The reddish-brown deposit formed on iron objects is known as **rust**. The process of formation of the reddish-brown, flaky substance on the surface of iron objects in the presence of moisture and oxygen (air) is called **rusting**.

▲ Rusting of iron

During this process, iron metal reacts with oxygen in air in the presence of moisture (water vapour) to form hydrated iron oxide or ferric oxide. Rusting is a slow and undesirable chemical change as it takes place over a period of time and weakens the strength of iron objects, thus making them brittle.

The chemical reaction of rusting can be represented as:

Iron (Fe) + Oxygen (O_2) + Water (H_2O) ⟶ Rust (hydrated iron oxide, $Fe_2O_3 \cdot xH_2O$)

Activity 4

Aim: To prove that rusting occurs in the presence of oxygen and moisture

Materials: Some iron nails, three test tubes, three corks, oil, water and anhydrous calcium chloride

Procedure:

1. Take three test tubes and put one iron nail in each of them.
2. Fill the first test tube with tap water.
3. Fill the second test tube with boiled and distilled? Add a layer of oil on top of the water.
4. Add some anhydrous calcium chloride in the third test tube.
5. Plug all the three test tubes with cork.
6. Observe the nails after three weeks.

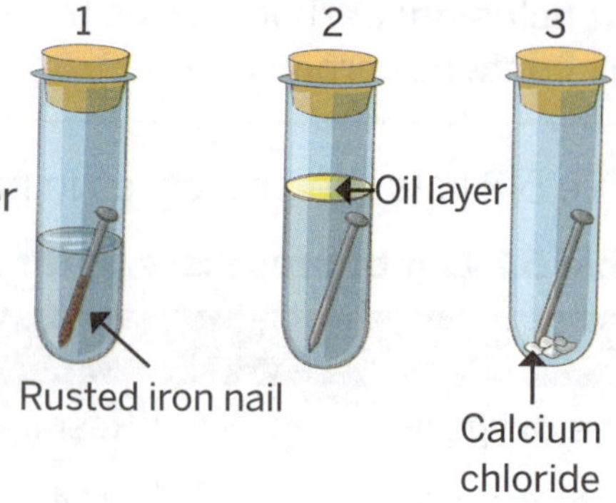

Observation: The nail that was placed in the first test tube rusted, while the other two iron nails did not rust.

Conclusion: In the first test tube, the iron nail rusted as there was air and water in the tube. In the second test tube, the iron nail did not rust as there was only water and the layer of oil prevented air from coming in contact with the nail. In the third test tube, the iron nail did not rust as the anhydrous calcium chloride absorbed moisture from the air. This proves that both air (oxygen) and moisture are required for rusting.

Conditions Necessary for Rusting

The presence of oxygen and water (moisture) is necessary for the process of rusting.

Methods to Prevent Rusting

Rusting may damage bridges, ships, etc., as these are made of iron. Hence, rusting should be prevented by stopping iron objects from coming in contact with moisture and air. This is done by following any of these methods.

- **Painting**: A layer of paint is applied to prevent the metal from coming in contact with air or moisture.
- **Electroplating**: The process of coating iron objects with metals that do not corrode is called electroplating. Metals like tin, nickel and chromium are used for electroplating which prevent rusting of iron.
- **Applying grease or oil**: A layer of grease or oil is applied on metals to prevent them from coming in contact with air and moisture.
- **Galvanization**: The process of coating iron objects with a thin layer of zinc metal is known as galvanization. Zinc is a corrosion-resistant metal. Hence, it prevents rusting.
- **Alloy formation**: Iron is mixed with corrosion-resistant metals like nickel and chromium to form alloys. Stainless steel is one such alloy. It is rust resistant. Hence, it is used to manufacture cooking utensils.

Do You Know?

The iron pillar in Delhi near Qutub Minar, built about 1600 years ago, has not rusted even till today. The monument has attracted many scientists and metallurgists from all over the world due to its unique feature.

Atmosphere

A thick layer of air surrounds the Earth. This blanket of air is known as the **atmosphere**. The atmosphere protects the Earth from the harmful ultraviolet radiations of the sun. It is about 480 km thick, but it gets thinner as the altitude or height increases from the surface of the Earth.

The atmosphere is made up of five layers: troposphere, stratosphere, mesosphere, thermosphere and exosphere.

Troposphere: It is the layer closest to the Earth's surface. It extends up to 17 km from the Earth's surface. The clouds that we see appear in the troposphere. As the altitude increases, the temperature of this layer decreases.

Stratosphere: It lies above the troposphere, from about 17 to 50 km from the Earth's surface. The ozone layer is a part of the stratosphere. The ozone layer is an important layer as it protects living things on Earth from the dangerous ultraviolet rays of the sun.

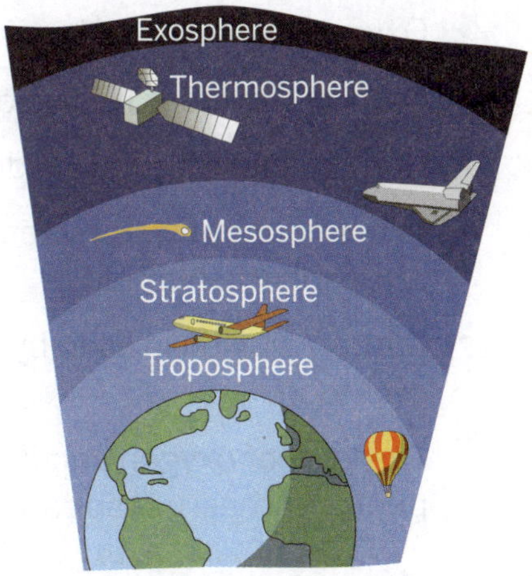

▲ Layers of atmosphere

Mesosphere: It extends from about 50 to 85 km above the Earth's surface. Meteors burn in this layer and we see them as shooting stars. As the altitude increases, the temperature and pressure of the layer decrease.

Thermosphere: It extends from about 85 to 500 km above the Earth's surface. Satellites and the International Space Station orbit the Earth in this layer.

Exosphere: It is the outermost layer of the atmosphere. It is present 500 km above the Earth's surface. Temperatures are very low in this layer.

The atmosphere helps to maintain a suitable temperature on Earth for organisms to survive. Without the atmosphere, our planet would be extremely cold! It also supports the water cycle, as it carries water vapour and formation of clouds and rain occurs here.

Keywords

Respiration: A process that involves breakdown of food (glucose) in the presence of oxygen to release energy

Combustion: A process that involves burning of a substance in the presence of oxygen with the release of heat and light energy

Fuel: A substance that can undergo combustion to produce heat and light

Photosynthesis: A process occurring in green plants in which carbon dioxide and water react in the presence of sunlight and chlorophyll to produce food and oxygen

Rusting: The process of formation of a reddish-brown, flaky substance on the surface of iron objects in the presence of moisture and oxygen

In a Nutshell

- Air consists of 78 per cent nitrogen, 21 per cent oxygen and the remaining 1 per cent consists of carbon dioxide, inert gases, water vapour, dust and smoke.
- Nitrogen is the most abundant gas present in the atmosphere.
- Oxygen is the second most abundant gas in the atmosphere.
- Carbon dioxide is released during respiration and combustion.
- Human activities have led to an increase in the amount of dust and smoke in the atmosphere.
- The amount of water vapour present in the air in a particular place is known as atmospheric humidity.
- Carbon dioxide is used by green plants in the process of photosynthesis to prepare their own food.
- The level of oxygen and carbon dioxide is balanced in nature mainly by the processes of photosynthesis, respiration and combustion of fuels.

Exercise

1 Choose the correct answer for each of the following.

a. The second most abundant gas present in the atmosphere is

i. oxygen ii. carbon dioxide
iii. nitrogen iv. water vapour

b. Certain bacteria present in soil can convert atmospheric ____________ into usable compounds.

i. carbon dioxide ii. nitrogen
iii. oxygen iv. water vapour

c. Green plants make use of ____________ during the process of photosynthesis to prepare their own food.

i. carbon dioxide ii. oxygen
iii. nitrogen iv. argon

d. Which of the following is a solid fuel?

i. Diesel ii. Wood
iii. LPG iv. Petrol

e. Oxygen is constantly replenished by green plants through the process of ____________.

i. photosynthesis ii. respiration
iii. sedimentation iv. combustion

f. Which of the following measures helps in maintaining the balance of oxygen and carbon dioxide in nature?

i. Discourage carpooling
ii. Encourage cutting down of trees
iii. Use of fossil fuels like petrol and diesel
iv. Use of cleaner fuels like CNG

g. Which of the following metals is used for electroplating?

i. Sodium ii. Tin
iii. Magnesium iv. Calcium

2 Fill in the blanks.

a. Meteors burn and appear as shooting stars in the ____________ (thermosphere/mesosphere).

b. ____________ (Carbon dioxide/ Nitrogen) is the most abundant gas present in the atmosphere.

c. Nitrogen ____________ (supports/ does not support) combustion of fuels.

d. ____________ (Argon/Radon) is used in the treatment of cancer.

e. Burning of fossil fuels releases ____________ (nitrogen/carbon dioxide) into the atmosphere.

f. Rusting of iron objects makes them ____________ (strong/brittle).

3 Write T for True and F for False.

a. Inert gases are very reactive in nature.

b. Humidity is high in coastal regions.

c. Oxygen is required for obtaining energy from food.

d. During combustion, only dust is released.

e. Petroleum fuels are cleaner fuels as they release less pollutants during combustion.

f. Carbon dioxide supports the process of rusting.

g. Painting iron objects prevents them from rusting.

4 Define the following terms.

a. Atmosphere

b. Toposphere

c. Atmospheric humidity

d. Combustion

e. Fuel

f. Photosynthesis

5 Differentiate between the following.

a. Respiration and photosynthesis
b. Liquid fuels and gaseous fuels
c. Electroplating and galvanization
d. Troposphere and thermosphere

6 Answer the following questions in brief.

a. What is the percentage of oxygen present in the air?
b. What are inert gases? Give examples.
c. What are the causes of increase in dust and smoke in the atmosphere?
d. What is the role of denitrifying bacteria in nitrogen cycle?
e. Write the word equations for:
   i. combustion of fuels.
   ii. photosynthesis in plants.
f. Why is CNG replacing petroleum fuels in automobiles?
g. Name the two main processes that help to maintain oxygen–carbon dioxide balance in nature.
h. What are the conditions necessary for rusting to occur?
i. What is rust? Write the chemical reaction involved in its formation.

7 Answer the following questions in detail.

a. Write a note on the composition of air. Also mention the volume (in percentage) of each component in the air.
b. How will you prove that oxygen is necessary for burning?
c. How do both plants and animals obtain nitrogen for their needs?
d. Explain the role of oxygen in respiration and combustion processes.
e. What are fuels? Explain their different types with examples.
f. Explain the importance of carbon dioxide for plants.
g. How is the amount of oxygen and carbon dioxide balanced in nature? Explain.
h. What are the factors that lead to oxygen–carbon dioxide imbalance in nature? Write a few measures to prevent this.
i. Explain the process of rusting and methods used to prevent it.

8 Think and answer.

a. What will happen if the percentages of dust and smoke increase in the atmosphere?
   (Hint: Recall the effects of dust and smoke on humans.)
b. On a rainy day, as soon as Amit came out of his air-conditioned car, his spectacle glasses became foggy. Why?

9 Project

Depict the composition of air in the form of a pie chart and write the importance of each component with images. Display it on your class notice board.

10 In the Library

a. Air consists of inert gases such as helium, argon, neon and krypton in small amounts. These gases are inactive. Collect information on the percentage of each gas in the atmosphere and their uses.
b. Carbon dioxide is present in less quantity in the atmosphere. Even if the percentage is slightly increased, it leads to global warming. Study more about global warming and its effects.

Worksheet

1 Subject Integration

All living things depend upon air for their survival. Animals need oxygen (O_2) for respiration and plants need carbon dioxide (CO_2) for photosynthesis. Write down how the levels of CO_2 and O_2 are maintained in the atmosphere and represent it in the form of a flowchart. Also, mention other means/processes that contribute to maintain the level of these two gases in the atmosphere.

2 Life Skills

Bursting fire crackers during festivals and functions increases the level of air pollution. China, India and other developing countries are the global contributors to air pollution. More than two-thirds of deaths happen because of air pollution. Release of toxic gases into the atmosphere causes asthma, bronchitis and other respiratory diseases.

Air pollution can be prevented by taking simple initiatives like travelling in the school bus instead of your parents dropping you to school using their own car or bike. Another way is carpooling and use of bicycles to travel small distances. This saves fuel and reduces pollution. Also ask your parents to get the emission test for their vehicles done, and use the vehicle if the test results are within the normal values.

Write two more preventive measures that can be taken to reduce air pollution.

____

____

Assessments

Assessment 1 (Chapters 1–3)

Marks: 40

1 Choose the correct answer for each of the following. (5 × 1 = 5)

a. Gases can be compressed and stored in cylinders because the ________________.

i. molecules are tightly packed
ii. intermolecular force is strong
iii. molecules are very loosely packed
iv. molecules cannot move freely

b. Which of the following metals has 'K' as its symbol?

i. Phosphorus
ii. Potassium
iii. Sodium
iv. Nitrogen

c. Which of the following methods is used to remove bran from wheat flour before making dough?

i. Sieving
ii. Magnetic separation
iii. Handpicking
iv. Filtration

d. Sublimation can be used to separate a mixture of

i. sand and ammonium chloride
ii. sand and sugar
iii. iron fillings and salt
iv. stones and rice

e. The main raw material used in the manufacture of detergents is

i. Oil
ii. Alkyl benzene
iii. Citric acid
iv. Phenol

2 Fill in the blanks. (5 × 1 = 5)

a. (Iodine/Ammonia) ________________ is a sublimable substance.

b. The process of conversion of liquids into solids upon cooling is called ________________ (sublimation/freezing).

c. Milk can be preserved by ________________ (pasteurization/salting) technique.

d. A (compound/ mixture)________________ is formed when two or more elements combine together chemically.

e. ________________ (Detergents/Soaps) are synthesized from petroleum products.

3 Write T for True and F for False. (5 × 1 = 5)

a. Elements cannot be broken down into simpler substances either physically or chemically.

b. Copper and gold are not malleable in nature.

c. Aspirin is also known as 'acetaminophen'.

d. Substances increase in size on both heating and cooling.

e. The process of conversion of solids into liquids upon heating is called vaporization.

4 Give reasons for the following. (5 × 2 = 10)

a. The symbol of sodium is Na.

b. When a room freshener is sprayed in one corner of the room, it can be smelled in the opposite corner of the room.

c. Use of sugar and salt as preserving agents.

d. Solids are hard and rigid.

e. Sublimation is a physical change.

5 Answer the following questions. (5 × 3 = 15)

a. Write a short note on the uses of chemistry in the field of food and medicine.

b. Explain the processes through which changes in states of matter occur.

c. Explain the principle and process of filtration. Mention the instances where filtration is used in daily life.

d. Write a short note on the process of sedimentation and decantation.

e. Explain the arrangement of molecules in solids, liquids and gases.

Assessment 2 (Chapters 4 and 5)

Marks: 40

1 Choose the correct answer for each of the following. (5 × 1 = 5)

a. Rainwater seeps down through the soil and gets collected to form ____________.

i. surface water ii. runoff water iii. groundwater iv. freshwater

b. Ozone is present in the ____________ layer of atmosphere.

i. thermosphere ii. stratosphere iii. mesosphere iv. troposphere

c. Identify the inert gas among the following.

i. Argon ii. Nitrogen iii. Oxygen iv. Carbon dioxide

d. Identify the method that helps to prevent water pollution.

i. Use of biodegradable fertilizers and pesticides

ii. Release of untreated industrial waste

iii. Wastage of water due to leaking taps at home

iv. Encourage the use of synthetic detergents

e. Which of the following is a solid fuel?

i. Diesel ii. Wood iii. LPG iv. Petrol

2 Fill in the blanks. (5 × 1 = 5)

a. In a salt solution, salt is the ________________ (solute/solvent).

b. The amount of water vapour present in the air in a particular place is known as ________________ (atmospheric humidity/clouds).

c. Meteors burn and appear as shooting stars in the ________________ (thermosphere/mesosphere).

d. A ________________ (spring/lake) is a source of groundwater.

e. The outermost layer of the atmosphere is ________________ (exosphere/troposphere).

3 Write T for True and F for False. (5 × 1 = 5)

a. The rate of solubility depends on the size of solute to be dissolved.

b. Diesel is a clean and cheap fuel as it releases fewer pollutants.

c. The percentage of nitrogen present in the atmosphere is 78 per cent.

d. All the water found on Earth is suitable for drinking.

e. CNG is compressed and stored in cylinders.

4 Give reasons for the following. (5 × 2 = 10)

a. Water is a universal solvent.

b. Dust and smoke are more prevalent in cities than in villages.

c. Excessive use of fossil fuels should be reduced.

d. The amount of water vapour present in the air is not constant in all places.

e. Carbon dioxide increases global warming on Earth.

5 Answer the following questions. (5 × 3 = 15)

a. Explain solubility and the different factors affecting solubility.

b. Write a short note on the different sources of water on Earth.

c. Explain the importance of carbon dioxide in photosynthesis.

d. What are fuels? Explain their different types with examples.

e. Mention the various ways of conserving water.